Beyond a Physical Disability

2001

The Continuum International Publishing Group Inc
370 Lexington Avenue, New York, NY 10017

The Continuum International Publishing Group Ltd
The Tower Building, 11 York Road, London SE1 7NX

Printed in the United States of America

Library of Congress Cataloging-in-Publication Data

Ayrault, Evelyn West, 1922–
   Beyond a physical disability: the person within—a practical guide
/ Evelyn West Ayrault
      p.   cm.
   ISBN 0-8264-1306-4 (alk. paper)
   1. Physically handicapped.   2. Physically handicapped—Psychology.
3. Developmental psychology.   I. Title.
HV3011   .A96   2001
362.4—dc21
                              00-069427

Material on Legal Implications, Traumatic Brain Injury, Mobility
Impairments, Speech Impairments, and Cerebral Palsy from the
Disability Resource Manual courtesy Columbia Basin College
Career Access, Department of Education, *www.cbcz.org*

Items from the Sammons Preston catalog reprinted by permission.

Beyond a Physical Disability

The Person Within—
A Practical Guide

Evelyn West Ayrault

Continuum

NEW YORK · LONDON

In memorial to

Gertrude A. Barber, Ed.D.,

whose sensitive understanding

and love for disabled people

made their lives so much easier

Contents

Why I Wrote This Book   13

Acknowledgments   17

1. Challenges Parents Face   19

Recognizing the Child Is Disabled   20

Rearing a Disabled Child Is Not Learned in College   21

Reactions of Relatives and Friends   21

Discovering Developmental Age Level   22

Pushing a Child Too Far Too Fast   24

Twelve Tips for Rearing a Handicapped Child   25

Suggestions for Making Your Child Socially Acceptable   25

Parents Should Cut Themselves a Break   26

Parents' Feelings Can Be Potent   27

Handling Stress   28

Coping with Emotional Pain   29

Parents of Nondisabled Children Need Understanding   30

What the Law Says   31

2. Challenges the Child Faces   33

Defining a Disability: The Earlier the Better   34

Home-Grown Attitudes   35

A Child Needs to Discover Himself   36

Playtime as a Therapeutic Time   38

How to Select Toys for Your Child   38

Doing Therapy at Home   45

Wrong Labels Can Condemn a Child   47

Should Disabled Children Be Disciplined?   49

What the Law Says   51

3. Challenges the Teenager Faces   53

A Good Self-Concept Is Important   54

How Parental Attitudes Influence Teenagers   55

What Is a Thin-Line Disability?   56

Adjusting to a Disability   57

Fears Common to Most Disabled Teenagers   59

Disabled Sibling versus Nondisabled Sibling   61

Important Personality Traits   63

Undesirable Personality Traits   65

Understanding Masculinity and Femininity   67

Mixing Femininity with a Disability   67

Mixing Masculinity with a Disability   69

The Disabled Teenager's Sexuality   70

What the Law Says   71

4. Challenges the Adult Faces   **73**

Combining a Disability With Adulthood   74

Stepping from the "Disabled World" into the Real
    World   75

Being Director of One's Own Life   76

Society's Reactions in Perspective   77

Stress Can Be a Dominating Problem   78

Are You a Second-Class Citizen?   79

Nondisabled One Day, Disabled the Next   80

An Inventory of Abilities Can Tell a Lot   82

What the Law Says   84

5. Challenges the Professional Faces   **96**

What Is Psychological Rehabilitation?   97

The Rehabilitation Team   99

Importance of Preserving Dignity and Modesty   99

Compatible Rapport Essential to Progress   100

Parents Should Seek Help   101

Behaviors That Can Challenge Professionals   102

What the Law Says   105

6. Getting Educated Is Possible   **106**

Importance of Early Education   107

Importance of a Sound Relationship between Teacher and
    Child   108

Parents' Influence on the Learning Process   108

After High School Graduation, What?   110

Is College for Every Disabled Person?   111

Making the Right Choice   112

Taking First Steps to College   114

Be Honest about Your Disability Traits   115

Facts College Students Should Understand   115

If Support Services Are Needed   124

What the Law Says   125

7. Life Can Be Made Easier   **127**

Taking Good Care of Oneself   128

Self-Care Abilities That Make Life Easier   129

Soap and Water Never Hurt Anyone   129

Grooming Can Improve Psychological Outlook   130

Too Much Makeup Can Detract   131

Suggested Adaptations of Personal "Tools"   131

Activities of Daily Living   131

Items Available from the Sammons Preston Catalog (Aids to
    Daily Living)   135

8. Joining the Work Force 144

The Giant Transition   145

Facing Realities in the Work Force   146

Forgoing the Job of Your Dreams   149

Importance of Self-Control   150

Financial Planning Is a Necessity   151

Needed! A Health-Care Program for the Disabled   153

Who Determines the Disabled Person's Future?   157

Appendixes 159

State Vocational Resources   159

Educational Financial Aid by State   164

Other Helpful Agencies   169

Why I Wrote This Book

This book may strike you as controversial. Although the book deals with many issues it does not address the problems of the mentally retarded, the deaf, or the blind. Rather, it deals with the problems faced by disabled children and adults with average or above-average intelligence.

Many of the problems physically disabled individuals face are rarely recognized and addressed by professionals. Due to the lack of this recognition, many professionals do not understand the scope of difficulties facing the individual. Therapists and counselors fear dealing with the embarrassment, anguish, and despair that a disability can impose on a disabled individual and his or her family.

I was reared by stern, unrelenting parents. I was not allowed to associate with disabled people. Even though I had Cerebral Palsy, my parents insisted that I behave like any other child. When it was time to go to summer camp for six weeks, I went to a camp for nondisabled children. When everyone my age took dancing lessons, I took dancing lessons. When my family went horseback riding on weekends, terrified as I was to sit on a horse, they insisted that I go too. Harsh as these requirements may sound, as I became a more seasoned psychologist, they became more understandable to me.

Those of us of average or better intelligence who are physically disabled can hold our place in society if we make certain adjustments. For instance, how well a disabled individual adjusts to life is determined by how successfully he or she adjusts to his or her physical disability. In my case, my parents were specific in their requirements. They did not intend to support me financially. They told me this in no uncertain terms after I graduated from high school. Upon college graduation they expected me to go out and look for a job like every other graduate. It made no difference to them that this would be quite simply more difficult for me to do than for the average graduate. "You are only as handicapped as you think you are. If you act like a handicapped person, people will treat you as one," my parents counseled me.

After receiving my masters degree in psychology and human development from the University of Chicago, without a nickel in my pocket, I started to pound the pavement looking for a job. One thing to my credit was that I was trained as a psychologist under the eminent Dr. Carl R. Rogers while I was at the University of Chicago. Rather than tell me that practicing as a psychologist might be difficult, Dr. Rogers told me that if I conducted myself in a controlled, dignified manner I should not have any trouble. I can still hear him say, "Evelyn, you can help people solve their psychological problems if you refrain from thinking about your own." To make sure that I understood what he meant, Dr. Rogers insisted that, as part of my training, I become a client of a counseling program that he directed at the university. Under his supervision, I matured as an individual and learned firsthand how it felt to be someone in a counseling environment. Such excellent advice from a master of therapeutic counseling has served me well over the years.

Rather than describe my disability in medical terms, you will get a better idea of me as a disabled individual if I list what I can and cannot do. For instance, never give me a tube of toothpaste with a cap off because when I grab it I squeeze it all out before it is ever put to use. I lack coordination in my hands. This prevents me from cutting my own foods or any other similar tasks. Picking up a cup of coffee is impossible for me. If I try, I will spill it all over the table and probably onto anyone else near me. Therefore, I never go anywhere without straws to drink through. I learned an embarrassing lesson when I began drinking wine, beer, and other assorted liquors through a straw. I learned the hard way that I should only *sip* through a straw when I indulge. The time I forgot to do this, I found myself under the table in a posh restaurant! Needless to say my date was not too happy with me. No wonder, he had a white clerical collar on.

I have assorted physical abilities. If the buttons are big enough, I have no trouble buttoning. No one has had to dress me since I was three years old. My mother made sure of this. It was not until two and-a- half years ago that I began using a wheelchair. In truth, I never would have dared to use one until both my parents were deceased. They would have had a fit! They prided themselves on the fact that their disabled daughter never had to be in a wheelchair. Until then I gallivanted around under my own steam. I traveled and, shopped in malls alone, and pushed a shopping cart (as a walker) up and down long hospital hallways in my work. Although the wheelchair has become a reluctant friend, I get about in it on my own.

I hope this book will help to persuade those in the rehabilitation field as well as general readers that a disabled child, teenager, or adult can reach a high level of normalcy. Most disabled individuals can do this if they are not pushed to do the impossible. For instance, to counsel a person that he must *accept* the fact that he may never walk, be able to drive a car, or be able to dance, can border on being cruel to him. Few people could easily *accept* such limitations. Ask yourself, could you accept the fact that you had one arm or one leg or one eye? Of course not. But, if realistically counseled, it is very possible that you could come to *adjust* to not having an arm, a leg, or both eyes.

Disabled people bristle at being classified as second-class citizens. It is degrading to them. If the disabled individual does not want to be classified as second-class, he should exhibit maximum emotional control, think of other people, and contribute what he can to society. (Throughout, I use "he" to refer either to he or she.) Second-class citizenry is not defined by how one walks, speaks, or physically handles oneself. Rather, it refers to how one behaves emotionally, socially, and intellectually. To avoid this classification, the individual should show respect for himself and take pride in everything he does. This will help him gain respect from others.

The first decision I made regarding my professional future was to correctly classify myself. Thus, I identify myself as *a psychologist who happens to be disabled*. I settle for nothing less and make a point of having my colleagues think of me this way. People often ask me if I feel that my disability has had a negative impact on my professional goals. If it has, I certainly am not aware of such an impact.

It took years of concentrated training and practice to fulfill Dr. Rogers's prospects for my success. Eventually, I became a seasoned clinical psychologist on staffs of some fine rehabilitation hospitals. In addition to this, I have run a full-schedule private practice. My clientele includes both disabled and nondisabled.

I approach my clients in an honest manner. My secretaries are trained to make sure that clients are told before they come into my office that I am disabled. I believe that to permit a client to discover this fact on his own would be unfair to the client.

Although some clients adjust immediately to my condition, others have difficulty doing so. If, after the initial consultation, a client shows signs of being uncomfortable in my presence, I do not hesitate to discuss the matter. If I determine that my disability is too distracting or upsetting to the client, I refer the person to a nondisabled psychologist.

Because I cannot write with a pen or pencil, of course I cannot take notes during counseling or testing sessions. Clients have told me that since I do not sit with a pad and pencil scribbling in front of them, they feel as if they have my total attention. To overcome this obstacle, I ask the person (or his family in the case of a child) if he would object to my recording his session. If he does, I then dictate my mental notes of the case to my secretary immediately after the session.

The way I write books is considered a horrendous chore by many. Since I cannot use a pencil or operate a computer keyboard, I compile my material by tape recording or dictating it to a secretary. Needless to say, this is not the easiest way to write a book. Since my secretaries are not with me twenty-four hours a day, there are many hours when notes for my book become impacted in my mind. Many are the mornings I arise with information packed like sardines in my head. I cannot begin working on it until one of my secretaries arrive.

Since this style of writing is a necessity in my case, there are times when my frustration levels rocket off the chart. It is frustrating to go over material that my secretary has transcribed and not be able to make corrections immediately. Many are the times that I put the work aside and have a glass of wine or go out with friends. There are other times when, after weathering writer's block, I am ready to have my thoughts put on paper but there is no one around to do it for me. By hook or by crook, eventually the books get written. This is my sixth. My seventh is to be the sequel to *Take One Step*, my autobiography. Its tentative title is *Taking Another Step*.

Acknowledgments

It takes many people to write and publish a book. No one knew this better than my agent, Sidney Kramer. I am indebted to him for introducing me to my editor, Evander Lomke. His sensitive and knowledgeable editorial skills made my job much easier. Without my two fine secretaries, Coleen Triana and Cassie St. Denny, I could not have completed this project. They really paid the price when I tested their patience with my constant requests for perfection. Thank you Coleen for your unrelenting time spent on the computer. Thank you, Cassie, for your skilled editorial, and phenomenal computer knowledge.

All of the examples in this book are based on real events that have happened to real people. Identifying information in the case histories discussed has been omitted to the extent that this has been possible.

E. W. A.

NORTH EAST, PENNSYLVANIA

CHAPTER 1

Challenges Parents Face

Challenges facing parents are awesome. They must exert maximum effort to handle them, or the problems can affect the whole family. Rather than give in to them, the best way to minimize their impact is to use them as a foundation on which to care for your child.

Most young people in love look forward to getting married, setting up housekeeping, and rearing children. Few anticipate having to bring up a disabled child. The possibility that a child of theirs could become disabled is furthest from their mind. If, for one reason or another, one of their children becomes disabled, their dreams of having a prefect family are shattered. The couple finds themselves in a tangled mess of emotions. They do not know where to turn or whom to go to for help. Feelings of happiness disappear and are replaced by feelings of anguish. Life has lost an aura of perfection.

The quality of the relationship between the parents is at stake. Each parent must work to save it. They must forthrightly evaluate themselves. Each must now ask: Do I possess what it takes to weather the many challenges? Am I willing to join forces with my partner to work for the benefit of our child? Only by honestly answering these questions will there be a chance that what was to be a perfect family can at least develop into a functioning family.

Special planning is necessary when there is a disabled child in the family. One major task is the drawing up of a special budget to cover medical costs and other treatment necessities. Engaging medical specialists and scheduling prescribed therapies must also be done. If the child is of school age, what school he is to attend must be decided.

No two parents react the same way. Whether the disability is minor or severe, and regardless of how it occurred, it still is a devastating experience for parents. How devastating depends upon the child's sex and birth order. If the child is a firstborn, the parents' reaction is more severe. When the disabled child is second or third in birth order, the parents' reaction is not as intense. Parents can console themselves by knowing their firstborn is undamaged.

Knowing that their child is disabled has a definite affect on each parent. For instance, research reveals that mothers identify more closely with a female child, and fathers with a male child. Thus, when a female child becomes disabled the mother's reaction will be more intense. Her dreams of easily being able to go shopping with her daughter, or eventually planning her wedding, are shattered. When a son is disabled, or becomes so, the father suffers more. Dreams of taking his son to sporting events, or having him work in the yard with him, are shattered.

How intensely a child's disability affects either parent cannot be measured. It makes it easier on both parents when communication between them becomes of paramount importance. Each parent needs to know how the other one feels. Even though the feelings may be negative, expressing them to each other can result in deeper understanding and bonding between them.

Recognizing the Child Is Disabled

Rearing a disabled child is stressful. It is a bewildering time for parents. The child presents them with a variety of problems, to say nothing of the worry the problems present. Some parents are faced with the worry of whether their child will walk, talk, or be able to interact in society. Feelings of disbelief and guilt dominate. Eliminating these feelings is difficult to do. Giving the parents a detailed definition of the disability can be helpful.

When parents do not understand the implications of the disability everybody in the family is affected. Everybody involved with the child's welfare needs to know all the implications. If the area of the brain governing speech is damaged, and the child is likely to have a speech impairment, everyone should know about this. If motor skills are damaged, possibly preventing the child from walking, feeding himself, or taking care of his personal needs, this should also be told. If the intellectual area of the brain is not damaged, above all, this should be made crystal clear. Parents need to know that just because a child is physically disabled that does not necessarily mean he is mentally disabled.

There are other heartbreaking realities that must be faced. For instance, it is important that parents realize that their child's disability can become more noticeable the older he becomes. For example, facial grimaces can become more conspicuous. Speech impairments can become more pronounced. The drooling of a five-year-old, while somewhat acceptable at age five, becomes more noticeable when he reaches his teenage years. Toileting a six or seven-year-old is not as objectionable as having to toilet a fourteen or sixteen-year-old. At this age his sexuality is maturing, which can make toileting him an objectionable job for some teachers' aides and caretakers.

Rearing a Disabled Child Is Not Learned in College

After learning their child is disabled some parents have to ask themselves: Where do I begin? How do I teach him? The more severe the condition, the more questions there are to answer. Some techniques used when rearing an average child can be used when rearing a child with a minor disability. However, they often cannot be suitably adapted for use with the more involved child.

It is normal and healthy for parents to wish periodically that things were different. If they did not, they would be considered nonsensitive and nonfeeling. However, where a disabled child is concerned things may never change. While the child may show improvement, his physical abilities may never be perfect.

Whether the disability is a result of a birth injury or due to some other reason, parental anguish can be lessened if they seek professional advice. For parents to hope that a miracle can end their emotional pain is unrealistic. There are no miracles that change a disabled child into a nondisabled child and nothing is gained when parents go in search of the unobtainable. Concentrating on improving the child's condition is less emotional for all concerned. It does not raise false hopes.

Reactions of Relatives and Friends

It is not unusual for grandparents to react to a disabled child in the family. When a grandchild is born disabled or becomes disabled after birth, grandparents join the child's parents in grieving. They may first experience denial that can be even stronger than that expressed by the parents.

Other family members and friends can hinder the parents' ability to cope. Some cannot handle the situation. Others are embarrassed. Still others express pity. In the final analysis, all types of family and friends ignore the disabled child and his family in an effort to make themselves feel more comfortable. When there is a family or social gathering they are not invited. If, on occasion, the family brings the disabled child to social gatherings, everyone treats the family timidly. No one knows what to say. Everyone fears he may say the wrong thing. Everyone wants answers to questions concerning the disabled child.

One family had a unique idea. After their child was diagnosed, they bought small cards, wrote the diagnosis on them, and sent them to their relatives and friends. At the bottom of each card they added, "Do not be afraid to ask questions." This helped to mellow the interaction between the parents of the disabled child, relatives, and friends. No longer did relatives and friends feel uncomfortable. An easy give and take relationship allowed them to ask questions clarifying the meaning of the child's condition.

Discovering Developmental Age Levels

Some disabled children have different developmental age levels. The variability of the age levels depends upon the type and severity of the disability. A child who is mildly disabled can have the same levels as the average child. The child who is severely involved will have assorted age levels. At the age of eight, he may have an educational age level of five years, a social age level of three years, and so forth. As a rule, parents are not informed of their child's developmental age levels.

An inventory of the disabled child's developmental ages realistically informs parents of developmental potential. For example, a six-year-old child may have difficulty washing his face with a washcloth and a bar of soap. However, if he is given a mitt, he does not have to worry about having the soap slip out of his hand. This adaptation makes it possible for him to perform the same activity as a nondisabled six-year-old. Without the adaptation, his face would have to be washed for him, which would give him the physical age of a three-year old.

Before evaluating a severely involved child it is important to determine what his various age levels are. When this is not done it is difficult to discover the innate abilities of the child. Following is a brief definition of each age level:

Mental Age: This is the level of development in intelligence that the child has reached at his chronological age level. The fourteen-year-old can have a mental age equal to his birth age or the mental age of someone older or younger than himself.

Physical Age: This is the ability to perform physical activities expected of a child at a given age level. If a fifteen-year-old boy can only partially walk by himself, sit up by himself, or feed himself then his physical age is not equal to his chronological age.

Emotional Age: This age level refers to a child's emotional development. If a teenager has an average IQ and is able to care for himself, but gets emotionally upset when things do not go quite his way, his emotional age may be below his chronological age. Two unmistakable signs of retarded emotional age are: emotional dependency on parents and fear of being away from home without a parent.

Educational Age: This is the determination of the grade level at which the child functions. This level is known as the educational age and is an indication of where the disabled child functions in relation to the average boy or girl his age.

Social Age: This category concerns itself with the child's level of social development in comparison with others his age. It is an indication of how he reacts among other people and whether he can maintain a relationship with them.

Most ten-year-olds get about by themselves under their own steam. If a child is unable to walk, he cannot do this. However, this need not mean that he cannot get about like the average child. He may have to use a different technique for doing so. For example, his method of getting about may be limited to the use of a wheelchair, use of crutches, or under his own steam but at a slower pace. In other words, both children get about. How they do it is not the point. The point is that the disabled child and the nondisabled child do the same thing. Therefore, if an inventory asks whether a child can get about by himself, and he does so with crutches or in a wheelchair, he should be scored a plus on the evaluation sheet. In other words, he does get about by himself, but differently from the average child.

The results from a developmental inventory can be of significant help to rehabilitation personnel. They can serve as a foundation for planning a therapeutic program. Being knowledgeable of a child's various developmental age levels can help determine which therapies should be given. For instance, if a child's physical age level falls at the eighteen-month line, and he is twelve-years-old, perhaps it would be better to concentrate on development of simple skills that fall at his chronological age level.

Pushing a Child Too Far Too Fast

Parents often push their disabled child beyond his capabilities. This can result in psychological problems. The child is apt to develop a poor concept of self or refuse to cooperate altogether with rehabilitation specialists. The case of twelve-year-old Carol is a good example. Her mother's desire to have her perform socially like other girls her age became an obsession. She was determined that Carol keep up with everybody else.

If Carol expected to be a part of the household she was to do chores like everybody else. Her poor hand coordination and stumbling walking gait were not to interfere. Carol's job was to set the dinner table every night. Lining up each piece of silverware evenly at the edge of the table was hard for her. Every time she put a piece of silverware evenly on the table, her arm would give an involuntary jerk and send the silverware flying in every direction.

Carol's frustration knew no bounds. In anger, she would pick up the pieces of silverware and throw them across the room. She had to repeat setting the table several times before she did it well enough to please her mother, whose intentions were well-meaning. However, by not recognizing how difficult it was for Carol to set the table all good intentions were canceled out. More would have been gained if Carol had not been pressured to do a perfect job. Had she been encouraged to set only one place setting per day until she built up some ability to do the whole table it would have been less frustrating to both Carol and her mother.

A child's concept of himself is marred when he is forced to perform beyond his abilities. Chances are that the parent is doing it to satisfy his own ego. He gives little attention to whether the child can perform the task or not, or how difficult it may be for him. The adage "if at first you don't succeed try, try again" is the motto of many parents. They can erroneously believe that repeating an activity over and over again will result in perfect performance.

Twelve Tips for Rearing a Handicapped Child

(1) Give your child a feeling of physical and emotional security.

(2) Accept, and respect your child.

(3) Help your child reach his maximum level in physical and emotional development.

(4) Encourage your child to be self-dependent and to accept what responsibility he is able to assume.

(5) Give your child the gift of emotional security by responding to him with patience and understanding from earliest childhood.

(6) Be consistent in all areas of development (discipline, feeding, home-bound treatment, etc.).

(7) Minimize fears and frustrations.

(8) Refrain from pushing your child beyond his physical and mental capabilities.

(9) Recognize that your child's wishes, opinions and ideas are evidences of his growth.

(10) Show a genuine interest in your child's accomplishments, however small they may appear to you.

(11) Praise your child for what he accomplishes.

(12) Encourage your child to accept himself as he is rather than as he wishes he were.

Suggestions for Making Your Child
Socially Acceptable

Neatness and Cleanliness

(1) Keep his clothes washed and well pressed.

(2) Keep his shoes polished and repaired.

(3) Promptly replace missing buttons on all clothing.

(4) Dress your child in bright, attractive clothing, easy to get on and off. Make him look attractive and perky in his clothes.

(5) Bathe him well at least once a day.

(6) Use talcum powder to keep him sweet smelling.

(7) Keep his teeth brushed and well taken care of.

(8) Use a fragrant soap when washing his face if he drools a lot. This prevents any stale saliva odor around the face and neck area.

Social Gestures

(1) Teach a boy to remove his hat when coming in off the street.

(2) Train the child to sit quietly in a chair when told to and not to pat or touch other people unless asked to.

(3) Train the child not to touch things in strange surroundings.

(4) Teach the child to ask to go to the bathroom quietly.

(5) Teach the child not to bang his feet or hands to attract the attention of adults who are in conversation.

(6) Teach the child such social phrases as: *Thank you. No thank you. Please. How do you do. How are you. Come again. I had a nice time. Good-bye. May I? May I have some? Your turn next. Play with mine. Please, and so on.*

(7) Teach the child his name and address, his age, where he lives, the day, month and year. Have him learn to say what games he plays, the names of any brothers or sisters, his father's name and perhaps the kind of work he does.

Your attitude is important

(1) School yourself to accept your child when you are out in society.

(2) Do not shelter him too much. Let him roam a bit in stores, under your watchful and not too obvious eye.

(3) Act as though you have every right to have your child out with you.

(4) If you are questioned about him, be as unemotionally matter of fact as you can in your answer. Tell the truth in a voice and tone that convey love. Your listener will take his cue from you and be less emotional and awkward about the matter.

(5) Every parent has a responsibility toward his child. Yours is to train him. If you do so intelligently, patiently and diligently, you are meeting his needs as fully as the parent who prepares his child for college.

Parents Should Cut Themselves a Break

The minute a child becomes disabled, attention centers exclusively around him. Gifts are brought and endearing remarks are made. The parents' reaction is given only secondary attention. The fact that it is the parents who must rear and train the child is totally ignored by nearly everybody in the family. If parents are to care for the child adequately, they have to be emotionally prepared to do so. Such ability is not obtained overnight. Parents must make a point of controlling their feelings, which will be difficult to do. Such feelings are rarely interlaced with happiness.

It is normal for parents to feel they have lost control over their lives. Being overwhelmed with "special" responsibilities can cause such a reaction. To be on constant call should the child have a convulsion, fall down, or exhibit uncontrollable behavior is an unnatural demand for most parents. For parents to get irritated, feel pressured, and want to run away from it all is a normal reaction.

In cases where the child has many demands, parents have little time for themselves. If they are to have any free time, they must make it available. Society will not do it for them. The public is adamant that the parents take good care of the child. That the parent might cut himself a break and take time off for freedom from the chore of handling the child is often cause for critical remarks from relatives and friends. Yet, if a parent does not allow special time for himself, away from the child, he will burn out and be worthless as a parent and caregiver. The best advice given to a parent is to cut himself a break and leave plenty of margin in his daily routine to satisfy his own need for relaxation.

Parents' Feelings Can Be Potent

Parents react with an overwhelming sense of loss when they are told their child is disabled. Some parents go through episodes of denial and go in search of an optimistic diagnosis or prognosis. Invariably, they are never told what they want to hear. The doctor's efforts at helping such a parent sometimes can be in vain. Trying to reason with them is difficult. The impact from the information given to them, by the doctor temporarily controls their powers of reason. They become nervous and apprehensive about everything. They get angry with each other, with the doctor, and with their insurance companies.

Another emotion that occurs is depression. Parents' feelings of depression become evident as they struggle with stress, acquiring enough energy to handle appointments, and the twenty-four hour care of the child. Depression is also enhanced if the parents argue over such issues as the diagnosis.

Feelings of guilt can also wreak havoc. This is particularly true where the mother is concerned. If her baby is born disabled, she frequently feels guilty because she did not bring a normal baby into the world. This is not an unusual reaction. The motherhood category is a fundamental part of any woman's feelings of worth. The emotional satisfaction a mother has when looking into the face of a normal, healthy newborn cannot be matched.

It is an entirely different experience for the mother who learns she has given birth to a disabled child. Her child's future is questionable. As she looks into the baby's face she sees nothing but unanswered questions and overwhelming problems. The category of motherhood is damaged and her sense of worth is shattered.

Intense feelings of emotional turmoil become even more evident when the doctor attempts to define the child's disability to the parents. They find themselves in a position the average parent never experiences. A doctor is spouting off medical terms they have never heard before. Understanding their meaning is impossible. What is being said to them by the doctor becomes colored by their feelings of depression. It all becomes a mishmash in their minds.

Parents should be encouraged to adjust to their child's condition. Suggesting that they accept it borders on being unrealistic. The negative connotation of being told to accept a child's disability is more than most parents can tolerate. Adjusting to the disability has a more positive implication. Being told to adjust to the child's disability does not require that the parents exhibit an unusual amount of personal fortitude. Instead it leaves avenues of thought open for executing positive actions.

Handling Stress

Stress is the most potent feeling parents experience. It breeds depression, grief, and anger. It comes between marriage partners. Parents must be aware of how stress can affect them. It is they who must be empowered to control it in their lives. They are the ones who know how much stress they can withstand.

Finding ways to free oneself from stress is not easy. The main requirement calls for the individual to change patterns of thinking. Engaging in an activity that he enjoys, which has no connection with the stressful situation in his life, helps to control negative thinking. Taking an "inventory" of what activities must be accomplished in a given period of time is good sense. If the child's care results in tense feelings for a parent (usually the mother) taking time out to do an activity she enjoys can counteract this.

If a mother has her hair done, has a manicure, or goes out to dinner with her partner, it can do much to reduce her feelings of stress. Although these activities are stress free, they mean nothing unless the individual can bring himself to relax physically and mentally. For instance, nothing is gained if one feels compelled to call home two or three times during an evening out to make sure the disabled child is all right. This is giving in to feelings of guilt, a basic ingredient of stress.

Fathers are spared much of the stress connected with rearing a disabled child. They leave the house every morning to go to work. It is the mother who is left behind to cope with the stress. For a her, stress is a whole different situation. She does not have the choices the father does. It is more difficult for her to make the decision as to whether to stay at home or go out and get a job. Yet, if she can accept a full-time or part-time job it can be a means for her to handle stressful feelings. Even if the salary earned has to go toward a babysitter, in the final analysis it will be money well spent.

Time and time again the author has recommended that mothers seek employment. This frees them from their stressful environment for a few hours each day. It raises their self-esteem and provides her with new feelings of competency. As she reevaluates herself she thinks better of herself. Being paid a salary for her efforts on a job does much to increase her sense of self-worth.

Coping with Emotional Pain

There is a difference between emotional pain and physical pain. Emotional pain is unseen but severely felt. Physical pain is both seen and felt. It is understandable that efforts are made to relieve physical pain. It is difficult to understand why efforts are not made to relieve emotional pain. Emotional pain is personal. Most people find it difficult to show how they feel. Being depressed or displaying tears over a disturbing situation is very embarrassing for them. Therefore, they keep the pain pent-up within themselves.

Many human reactions make up emotional pain. Feelings of depression, anxiety, fear, and despondency are all included. Parents can be victims of any one of these feelings, or be victims of all of them. Throughout the parents' lives, the life of their child, and the duration of the disability, emotional pain is a constant element. Even though the impact of the pain may lessen in time, it never leaves. It is triggered every time the parent looks at the child.

Communication is a primary remedy that can help heal pain. This can only take place, however, if parents honestly identify the source of their emotional pain. To do this it is essential that they are allowed to express freely how they feel to each other. Pent-up feelings exaggerate emotional pain. Similar to champagne in a bottle, if the cork is not removed, the shaken bottle will explode. The same is true of a human being. If he is not allowed to express his feelings freely he will, like a popped cork, explode.

When there is no communication in partnerships, emotional pain increases. If a wife does not feel free to express her inner emotional pain to her husband, it will grow in intensity. If the husband does not feel free to tell his wife his inner emotional pain it will increase also. Parents who cannot interact with each other are parents who are in denial. Such parents cannot live comfortably with the fact that their child is disabled. Parents who to try to do so are being unrealistic about their human capacity. They can only handle so much without professional guidance. Being allowed to speak one's mind is the best healing process.

Parents of Nondisabled Children Need Understanding

The problems of the disabled child not only affect his parents, but also the parents of the nondisabled child. These parents have a right to speak up on behalf of their child. While they are sympathetic to the problems concerning raising a disabled child, it should not be overlooked how these problems can affect the able child. To want their child not to be in continuous contact with a disabled one is a normal impulse. Some parents fear their child will "catch" the disability. Others fear there is a stigma attached from associating with such a child, and it will hurt his future social standing.

Should both children be in the same classroom, special problems can arise. The teacher's time can be taken up with meeting the needs of the disabled child. The nondisabled child then is deprived of the teacher's attention. This can be of grave concern to his parents. Of even more concern are the types of behavior the disabled child exposes the other child to. Watching a disabled classmate have a grand mal seizure three times per day can be frightening. Placing all concern on the welfare of one child over the other is not acceptable. The teacher should divide time evenly between the disabled child and his able classmates. How healthy it is for the nondisabled child to be in constant contact with the disabled child is questioned by some professionals.

Solutions must be worked out for the benefit of each child. The nondisabled child should be provided with time to function without the disabled child tagging along. If he wants to run around the ball field or join a sports team, he should be able to do so without feelings of guilt. In essence, he needs space in each day when he can function as a nondisabled youngster.

A plan should also be worked out for the disabled child. He needs to function at his own rate of speed and not feel he is in competition. As he enters his teenage years he must understand why his able peer needs to get away from him. Likewise, he needs to get away from the nondisabled peer and do his own thing. One should not be placed at the mercy of the other. The association between the two should be equal.

Counseling sessions provide an opportunity for parents of both the disabled and nondisabled child to express their concerns. Nothing is gained if one or the other feels that he should hold back his emotions. The parent of the disabled child should be made aware that the parent of the nondisabled child fears not only for himself, but for his child as well.

Parents of the disabled child also need a break. They need space to express their feelings. They need to feel free to vent their anger and envy toward the other parent. If they wish to state, "You better feel grateful. You better thank God you are not in our situation," they should feel free to say so. It is only when each parent can adjust to the true feelings of the other that the disabled child will be accepted, and the nondisabled child will feel free to do the accepting.

What the Law Says

Awareness of the laws that ensure equal opportunities to individuals with disabilities is vitally important for the following reason:

Knowledge of the language and intention of the laws empowers families to advocate more effectively for their children and strengthens their ability to participate fully as partners in their children's educational teams.

As independence and self-sufficiency for individuals become increasingly important outcomes of special education, it is important that individuals with disabilities understand the laws and their implications for making decisions.

Knowledge of the laws can assist professionals in understanding the entire service delivery system, ensure protection of civil rights, and improve collaboration with other agencies and families.

Knowledge of the laws can help parents and professionals work together on behalf of children to make the equal education opportunity guaranteed by law a reality.

P.L. 93–380, The Family Education Rights and Privacy Act (FERPA)

This law, often called the Buckley Amendment, gives parents of students under the age of eighteen, and students age eighteen and over, the right to examine records kept in the student's personal file. The FERPA was passed in 1974 to cover all students, including those in postsecondary education. The major provisions of the Act are:

Parents and eligible students have the right to inspect and review the student's educational records.

Schools must have written permission from the parent or eligible student before releasing any information from a student's records. While a school may disclose education records without consent to others, such as other school officials, schools to which a student is transferring, certain government officials, and state and local authorities, the school must keep track, within the student's files, of the requests for these records. This information can be inspected by the parent or eligible student.

Parents and eligible students have the right to have the records explained and interpreted by school officials.

School officials may not destroy any education records if there is an outstanding request to inspect and review them.

Parents and eligible students who believe that information in the education records is inaccurate or misleading may request that the records be amended. The parent or eligible student must be advised if the school decides that the records should not be amended, and has the right to a hearing.

Finally, each school district must give parents of students in attendance, or students age eighteen or over, an annual notice to inform them of their rights under this law, and the right of parents or eligible students to file a complaint with the U.S. Department of Education.

CHAPTER 2

Challenges the Child Faces

The physically disabled child is challenged to make the most of his abilities every waking hour. He is challenged to discover what he can and what he cannot do. He is challenged to adjust to the uncertain feelings his disability causes him. The problems that make up his life are emotionally traumatic. For instance, watching a child with poor standing balance try to walk can stir anyone's emotions. Everybody waits for him to fall down. Even a nondisabled five-year-old is affected. He knows what it feels like to fall down and hurt himself. Thus, watching his friend lose his balance, the five-year-old instinctively jumps up to help him.

Determining how the child adjusts to his disability is important. Will he adjust emotionally? Or will the adjustment be in a controlled manner? The approach parents take regarding these questions can be a deciding factor as to how the child will progress over the years. He will be rejected by peers if he displays objectionable behavior. If he is ten-years old and acts like a five-year-old because he does not get his own way, playmates will classify him as a "baby." *Average children are rarely influenced by a child's disability. They react to erratic emotional behavior.* If the disabled child emotionally acts out, causing his disability to become more exaggerated, other children become frightened and will shy away from him.

Most children behave in public as they are allowed to behave at home. If they are allowed to rule the roost in the home, they will try to do the same in public. If they are treated with love and dignity, they will treat other people in the same way. This is just as true in the life of the disabled child. His home environment influences his behavior in society. If he is not trained to conduct himself in an acceptable manner at home, he will not do so in public. If he is allowed to demand attention from his family, he will demand attention from the public. If he is courteous to people who help him, he will be the same to people outside the home.

Defining a Disability: The Earlier the Better

The curiosity of every child runs the gamut. He is curious about himself and everybody around him. He wonders if he looks as good as other kids. He wonders if other kids will like him. He also wonders how the moon is lit, what makes it rain, and what makes the sun shine.

The physically disabled child is equally as curious. He wonders about everything. He wonders about himself. He wonders if other kids will like him. And, he wonders about his disability. Whether his disability is minor or severe, and regardless of how it was contracted, it makes him feel uncomfortable in the presence of other kids.

Failure to provide honest answers to the disabled child's questions can result in pent up feelings of depression. For a person of any age to spend hours, days, even years, trying to overcome the impossible can be a depressing experience. Anyone would have to have a strong constitution to keep from feeling defeated when they try and try again without success.

Due to the many drawbacks a disability can present, keeping depression at a minimum is not an easy task. One solution might be to provide the child with a simple definition of his disability. Providing this to a child who is four or five years old can have immeasurably positive results. It has been proven that the younger a child is given a task to learn, the more likely he is to learn it easily. This can also be true in the case of the young physically disabled child. The younger he is when the disability is defined to him, the less likely it is that he will spend hours, days, or years trying to accomplish feats he may never accomplish.

A ten- or twelve-year-old disabled child is old enough to understand a simple definition of his disability. To minimize to him the characteristics of his disability borders on being cruel. He has a right to know everything about his disability. It is right to prepare him for society's reaction. Furthermore, he has a right to know what physically he may or may not be able to do. If it is obvious he will never kick a football, or be able to ride a two-wheeled bike, the younger he is told this fact, the better it will be. He will be spared from trying over and over again only to fail at being able to kick the ball or ride the bike. Conversing with the physically disabled child in a straightforward manner is important. He is sensitive to what is said to him, and the tone of voice in which it is said. For instance, using such phrases as, "Maybe someday . . . ," or, "You will be able to do it . . . ," and other like phrases can be misleading. If the child is severely involved he needs to learn that if he cannot do a skill now, it is possible he may never be able to do it. While such brutal frankness may bring a tear or two, it can help spare the disabled child from building false hopes.

Twelve-year-old Joey's case is a good example. When he started asking his mother about his disability, she first consulted the author. This was a touchy subject for her to handle. She was aware that it also was a critical time in her son's life. In a preliminary conference with the mother, I made a point of determining for myself whether she had come to grips with the impact of her son's disability. Once she realized that Joey would be disabled for life, I then encouraged her to proceed with educating him about his disability.

Joey's mother began by pointing out to him that everybody is different. The person who wears glasses looks different from the person who does not. When Joey asked his mother if he would always have a disability, she told him yes, he would always be disabled. She explained that although he could improve as he got older, the disability would never go away. When he asked why his hands shook when he tried to button his shirt or brush his teeth, he was told that his ability to do things with his hands might get better as he grew older but would always shake.

Because Joey's mother was so honest with him, she provided him with valuable "tools" to function as a disabled teenager. Possessing such true information about his disability, he could tell his friends exactly what was the matter with him. This opened up many gates. His friends lost no time in asking him questions about his disability. His mother's simple definition became Joey's trademark. When new kids moved into the neighborhood and asked the other kids what was wrong with Joey, they were told to ask Joey himself. This satisfied their curiosity and they treated Joey as a regular kid.

Home-Grown Attitudes

Every child should develop feelings of personal worth. Where and how he does this depends upon how he is treated at home. Is he treated like a human being? If the home environment is tranquil, yes. If it is loud and unstructured, everybody in the family will be in turmoil. This can also be true in the home of the physically disabled child. If his family is adjusted to his disability, he will show this adjustment in his behavior. If, however, his disability causes hostility and anger between his parents, the opposite is true. It will have a definite affect on the child. His behavior will be unstable, excessively emotional, and he will act immaturely for his age.

The case of Mr. and Mrs. Jones vividly describes how parental attitudes can affect a child. They were determined to prove that what they were told by professionals about their eight-year-old son, Kenny, was not true. They had a great deal of difficulty adjusting to the fact that their son was brain-injured. They bristled at people who made suggestions on how to rear Kenny. For example, when it was suggested they place Kenny in a special school, they retaliated by saying, "He is not like those children. No son of ours will go to a class of dumbbells."

Kenny's father found it unusually difficult to adjust to his son's disability. When Kenny and his father ate out in public and people stared, he would jump up from his table, and angrily ask, "What are you looking at? My son is as good as yours!" This clearly did not set a good example for Kenny. It did little to help him adjust to his disability. Instead, Kenny got the idea that the best thing to do when people stared at him was to fight. Unfortunately, the father's reaction affected every relationship Kenny attempted to develop. When neighbor kids said that because he could not run fast enough he could not take part in their game, Kenny exploded in anger. As a result of such behavior, Kenny was not a popular friend.

A Child Needs to Discover Himself

Some relatively intelligent physically disabled children have trouble identifying parts of their body. This can be particularly true of the child with spastic paralysis. His arms and hands may be so tense that he cannot touch his legs or his hair, his ears, eyes, or nose. He may have a lot of trouble moving these limbs around. That he does have such difficulty can give a false impression of his basic intelligence. For example, one item on a psychological test requires a child to point to his ears, the back of his head, his knee, and his elbow. If he cannot do this he does not pass that portion of the test and must be given a minus score. However, this score is not valid if it is found that the child can name these various parts of the body. The fact that his tense muscles will not permit him to point to them is excusable. It is most likely that if he could easily move his arms and hands he would be able to point to his hair, the back of his head, his eyes, ears, and nose.

This is a classic example of how the initial physical abilities of a child can be undermined. It is important to take into account what affect a child's physical inabilities may have on his intellectual abilities. Frequently, it can be discovered that a child's intellect far exceeds that of his physical ability. Does a tense body limb prevent the child from performing a physical skill? For example, does a tense arm and hand prevent the child from picking up a glass of water and drinking it like any other child? In all likelihood, it does. However, it should not be taken for granted that the child cannot drink from a glass. Intellectually he may very well be able to do so. All he needs to do is to find another method for drinking from the glass. Rather than pick it up like the average child, the physically disabled child may find it easier to drink his water or milk through a straw. This is another example where a child's physical inability can be surmounted by introducing a substitute method for that inability.

The severely involved child's inability to make discoveries in the environment can have an affect on his intellectual, social, and emotional development. Not being able to identify his body parts is only one aspect. Not being exposed to other environmental subjects is still another aspect. Driving along in a car and not having things such as cows, airplanes, and even passing cars pointed out to him limits his intellectual knowledge. If the child is never told what animal gives us milk, or that we can travel in an airplane, chances are he will never accumulate such information. Most children have the opportunity to visit a farm, even travel on an airplane. Other children learn from going on field trips at school. Too often the disabled child is deprived of such experiences. Thus, if he is to acquire such information it must be brought to him by someone in his family. That he may not know such information is not a sign of intellectual retardation.

The importance of injecting the environment and all it contains into the mind of the disabled child cannot be overstressed. It should hold high priority in the list of learning activities. Not to provide it is to retard the child purposely. One of the first things I attempt to find out about a young, severely involved child is what experiences he has had outside the home. What knowledge has he been exposed to? Has he ever visited a farm or the zoo? Has the mother taken him shopping in the supermarket? Each of these areas can provide basic information to a child. He needs to know what an animal is. He needs to know where food comes from and that there are many different kinds of food. He needs to be exposed to shuffling back and forth in a crowd of people. This is how every child develops his basic foundation for information. If he cannot see or hear the different elements making up society, he will never know what they are and never know what it is to experience their feelings and sounds.

Playtime as a Therapeutic Time

If a child is so disabled that he cannot walk, does not speak clearly, or cannot endure long periods of general play, it may be necessary to introduce adaptations. However, this does not mean the child should just sit and watch, wishing he could do what he sees other neighborhood children doing. Play is an important part of every child's life. It has been found that play is a child's work. The disabled child's need for play is as great as any other child's. It introduces him to various kinds of activities. At play he can learn the feeling of things, how hard they are, how soft, how big and heavy, or whether they are round, square, or pointed. Playtime provides the disabled child with the opportunity to discover whether his ball or truck or crayon is red, blue, or yellow. Being deprived of these experiences stunts the child's development.

All at once discovering that he can roll a ball, maybe push a truck with his hand or foot, or perhaps make a mark on a paper with a crayon, provides the disabled child with a sense of control over his own abilities. Play can give him the opportunity to test his ideas and feelings and put them into action. He finds that with one toy he can do this and with another toy he can do something different. By so discovering, he is finding a difference in different toys, as well as having to make a decision as to which toy with which he wants to play. On the following pages is a list of toys that can serve as a helpful guide in making selections for the disabled child.

How to Select Toys for Your Child

Observe your child.
Play with him. Watch to see what he can do with his hands, arms, and fingers. Can he walk? Can he get about by himself? Is most of his time

spent sitting in a wheelchair? Does he understand directions? What seems to hold his interest?

Determine your child's play stage.

Your child may be at a single stage of mobility where he can simply grab an object or he may be at several stages where he can grab an object, transfer it from one place to another, put one thing down and grab a new object in place of it in the same hand. He may be in a transitional stage where he can only grab an object but is trying hard to develop the next step of transferring it from one hand to the other.

Select toys that serve several purposes.

To save storage space and also save money, concentrate on toys with multiple uses. For example, any doll would please a child, but a doll that can be dressed and undressed, buttoned and unbuttoned, fed and changed, can improve hand-eye coordination. And it is likely to improve speech as the child talks to it lovingly or admonishingly. A wobbly clown will make him laugh, and if the game is to blow him down, a child can get fine practice in the good lip and breath control required as preparation for intelligible speech.

Don't be guided by chronological age if your child is severely disabled.

A toy suitable for a younger or older child may be just right for your child in light of his physical limitations. For the same reason, he may continue to play with a toy long past the time a child his age normally would, because he can manage it well and adapt it for himself. In choosing toys, don't be limited by the suggested age. Select them with their developmental purpose in mind.

Choose toys that are sturdy and durable.

All children are dismayed when their toys break. The handicapped child is perhaps even more disturbed, concluding that it may have been his fault. Buy toys that are sturdy and will not shatter if dropped accidentally. If they are on wheels, be sure that they do not tip over easily. If the toy flies apart the minute your child touches it or hits it involuntarily with a flailing arm, he may become discouraged and lose his incentive to play with it.

**Pick attractive toys that motivate your child and create a
desire to play.**
Color is a part of the magic of toys, and bright colors do much to stimulate a child's interest. A child who is reluctant to make the effort to exert
himself and use his arms, hands, and legs and entertain himself, will
often respond to the allure of a bright toy. Keep this in mind when you
make your choice.

**Use toys to encourage your child to develop his best
muscular skill ability.**
Resist the temptation to insist that your child play with a toy as it was
meant to be played with. When he grows familiar with it and finds he
can manage it, he may be encouraged to handle it in a variety of ways.
This can improve his muscular skill ability.

Let toys help stimulate your child to express his feelings.
If your child has difficulty speaking intelligibly, this is important. Toys
that he can hammer on, clay he can knead, and dolls he can talk to can
serve as an outlet for him. A toy train, for instance, is often used by a
child to express his feelings. As he "choo-choo-choo's" away, the sound
gives him welcomed emotional release.

**Take advantage of the opportunity toys give
your child to socialize.**
Give normal children who are strangers to each other toys to play with
and they are soon friends, busily engaged in the activity before them.
Handicapped children have far fewer opportunities to have social experiences with other children. Be sure that your child has a few toys he can
occasionally share with two or three other children in his playroom. His
playmates will stimulate him to participate more than he might otherwise, and he will have the pleasurable experience of relaxing with
friends.

The toys suggested on the following pages should serve as a helpful
guide in making selections for your child and in suggesting gifts other
people may want to get him. Don't be afraid to improvise and don't feel
that you must get exactly the toy listed. You may find something along
the same lines that suits your child's need and interests better.

Therapeutic Aim of Toy	**Type of Toy**

1. Reach, Grasp, Release

To encourage and stimulate him to want to reach out.	Toys that dangle, move, are large, bright, and desirable. Any kind of toy that will move your child to want to reach out. Keys on a chain, bright cars, trucks, trains, balls, a shiny musical horn.
To encourage him to hold on to a toy if it is put in his hands.	Bright toys. Long, thin toys that have a pliable or hard handle section. Any object small enough to fit into the palm of the hand. Rattles, bells on handles, that can be held in the palm of the hand, loosely stuffed flexible animals.
To encourage him to reach out for and touch a toy even though he may not be ready to grasp it.	Throwable toys, toys that require slight manipulation, toys your child can grasp easily, hold and then let go. A spoon, stuffed dog, empty thread spool, blocks.
To develop his ability to open his hand and close it precisely.	Toys that can be squeezed, thrown, taken apart or stacked; any kind of toy that requires the child to grasp and then release a toy repeatedly. Toys that require him to open and close his hand. A soft rubber doll or animal that squeaks when squeezed; such games as toy bowling that require rolling a ball.

2. Thumb-and-Finger Grasp

To encourage him to use fingertips to lift his toys rather than grasp them with the palm of his hand.	Large toys he can stack, take apart, push. Lightweight objects that must be picked up with thumb and forefinger because of their particular size and shape. Blocks to stack on a wooden spindle, hand puppets, a harmonica, wooden take-apart toys, trains, or trucks.

To encourage him to use only a few fingers and his thumb.

Small stacking toys he can manipulate creatively. Crayons, wooden ABC blocks, a painting set and brush, games using checkers, minute doll furniture, pieces of colored ribbon or strips of colored art paper to be stuck on a felt board.

To make it necessary for him to use his thumb and index finger only.

Creative toys with very small parts he can take apart. Chinese checkers, large buttons to pick up and put in a cup or box.

To develop the fine use of thumb and index finger.

Toys and games he must hold, wind, construct or assemble. Toys with tiny parts. Toys that require that he make precise use of the tips of his thumb and index finger. Jack-in-the-box, winding toys, turning the pages of books, a pinball game; working with the zipper on a bag, picking up match sticks or tiny beads.

3. Finger Use

To encourage him to use fingers freely.

Toys, games, and activities are messy, creative, manipulative. Activities that motivate finger flexing, pressing, unrestricted movement of the fingers. A counting frame of colored beads, sand and water, flour and water mixture, finger paints, clay, finger games.

To improve the use of his individual fingers, particularly his index finger.

Toys, games and activities that require a lot of finger action. Any toy that needs precise use of a finger or placing, pressing or circulating motions. A toy dial telephone, a gun, puppets on a string.

To develop strength in his thumb so that eventually he can do activities requiring a fine dexterity.

Thumb toys requiring thumb action, thumb manipulation or any exact use of or pressing from the thumb.

Button puppets, pasting pictures on a large cardboard, doll snap clothesline, marbles, tiddlywinks, a toy cash register.

To stimulate the coordinated use of his fingers and to improve general dexterity in his whole hand.

Any activity using the hand in which fine finger coordination is required. Any activity that requires that all fingers move exactly at the same time. Activities that call for synchronized use of both hand and fingers. A stencil book, sewing colored yarn onto a square of cardboard, a tool chest, typewriter, toy piano, knitting toy.

4. Using the Arms Together

To encourage him to use both arms naturally, and to minimize any tightness in his arms, particularly at his shoulders and elbows.

Large, wide-area reaching toys, toys he must use his arms to reach for, throw or move in different directions. Toys to punch; a water and scrub board, swing, games using both hands and arms, a tricycle, boxing gloves.

To encourage him to use both arms, not just the one that is disabled.

Large holding toys that are lightweight and long, requiring a wide stretching motion of his arms, even if one arm is used more than the other. Two pot covers, a rolling pin, toy lawn mower, mixing bowl, and spoon to stir flour and water, batter, etc.

To help him develop the domnant (right or left) use of one hand only, but only if he is ready to do so.

Toys that are manipulative but also simple for him to use. Toys that are creative, constructive, hand-over-hand in natural situations. Toys he must hold in one hand while he makes them work with his other hand. Stringing beads, toys that hook together, a garden set, toy mailbox, house-keeping tools such as a mop or carpet sweeper, tinker toys.

To help him learn to use both hands, leading hand and helping hand in natural situations.

Fine-skilled manipulative toys that are creative and dramatic, and require a precise use of both hands. Any activity with his hands that calls for screwing, placing, matching or alternating motions. Paste paper, scissors, doll feeding equipment, hammer and nails, games requiring two people, washing doll clothes.

5. Hand–Eye Coordination

To help him develop gross arm control.

Toys that are nonrestrictive. Games that do not have to be held by a hand, but do need to be placed by a hand. Activities that offer some reward for success and no concern for failure. Toys that bob in bath water, a punch bag, finger paints, plastic balls suspended from the ceiling to be batted back and forth; simple painting of planks of lumber; rocking of doll cradle or baby carriage.

To help him develop the ability to use his arm and hand to place objects, even if he does so crudely and awkwardly.

Toys and games that require him to throw objects within a large area, a ball field, a play court, a given circle or square marked on the floor, beanbags into a bucket or wastebasket; coloring between drawn lines.

To develop maximum control in his arm.

Toys that he can readily tinker with, that interlock, that he can take apart; activities and toy skills in which the eye guides the hand to put a part in place. A toy construction set, puzzles, trains, cars or trucks that can be disassembled, kitchen pans and cups to stack.

To train the exact control and placement of his arm.

Any fine-skill toys that need placement or that he can construct. Any skill in which he has to exercise fine use of his hand, place things exactly, utilize fine hand-to-eye coordination. Simple pegboards, lacing a weighted high top shoe, jigsaw puzzles, a record player with a simple record arm, any household object that fits.

Doing Therapy at Home

Like any other child, the physically disabled child must be encouraged to develop to his maximum. To what degree he will develop depends upon the type and severity of the disability. In the majority of cases it requires therapy to be given, medication to be taken, and doctors to be consulted on a regular basis. How demanding all this is on the family will depend upon the child's age and the severity of his condition. If his disability is minor, the extra requirements will be few. If it is severe, consistent therapies, medication, and doctor visits will be necessary.

It can be disturbing to parents when they have to submit their child to regular therapy sessions. This, in the minds of classmates, can make a child appear more different from the average. Having to go to speech, physical, and occupational therapies three times a week can classify a child as unusual in the eyes of his classmates. When a therapist takes the disabled child out of the classroom for a half hour of therapy it is not missed by nondisabled classmates. It does not take them long to figure out that because their friend is different he must have special care. The average child's curiosity about this is normal.

The disabled child whose parents make sure that he gets enough therapeutic exercise in the home is indeed lucky. By being innovative about the therapy he needs, they spare him being classified as "different" by his nondisabled friends.

The case of Della is a good example. That she was physically disabled was enough of a heartbreak for her family. The fact that she also was being classified as "different" because she required so much therapy only added to their distress. Although she did have to go to therapy during the week, her parents made sure that her exercises at home were therapeutically geared.

The major concern to Della's parents at this time was that although she was five years old she had not started to walk. No child of theirs was going to spend his life in a wheelchair. To make sure this did not happen her parents bought Della her first tricycle. By learning how to ride, they hoped Della would get good leg exercise. Her feet were buckled to the pedals and her father insisted that she push down on one foot and then the other to make the tricycle go.

Della screamed with fright. She was afraid she would lose her sitting balance and fall off the machine. After her father gave her a couple of spanks on the fanny, Della got the idea of how to ride the tricycle. Once Della had built up confidence in herself and was able to push each pedal down, she became a speed demon on her tricycle.

Dancing lessons also helped Della. Ballet, toe-dancing, and tap dancing became loves of hers. To everyone's surprise it was discovered that Della possessed potential grace. The ballet dancing did much for her coordination. She soon was able to hold her arms out to the side and relax. Another dance exercise required Della to hold onto the dance bar with one hand and stretch one leg the length of the bar and then the other. Eventually she was able to do the splits and get up by herself from the floor. This indicated that her uncertain balance was becoming more certain.

Horseback riding proved to be another excellent source of exercise. It also did much to improve Della's coordination. After many hours of practice, she finally learned how to keep control of her hands. This was very important if she did not want the horse to go up on its hind legs and dump her on the ground, which would have happened had she pulled too hard on his mouth with the reins. The horse did buck Della off, once. It never happened again after she learned how to be gentle on the horse's mouth. The day she fell off the horse she was terrified. Fortunately, her riding master paid her fear little heed. He helped Della to get right back up on her horse. If he had not done this, Della would never have ridden a horse again. She spent some ten or twenty years riding horses.

Della's parents are to be commended for their innovative methods of physical therapy. Because of this, everything Della did helped her to improve physically. Her parents were against her going for any type of therapy. Their biggest fear was that it would indicate that Della needed something special that other children did not need. They refused to allow her to become a member of the disabled world. They believed strongly that if she were to be a member of society, then she must act like everyone else and do everything they did. This approach, however, must not be applied to every case. Parents who use such an approach must be in control of their own emotions and be able to help the child realistically perform, not necessarily for the parents' benefit.

Wrong Labels Can Condemn a Child

Using haphazard labels to identify a disabled individual is unwise. It can further emphasize the individual's disability. This happens when labels are used by persons who do not understand their meaning. When this happens to a disabled child, it can wrongly classify him. For instance, labeling an individual as a slow learner implies that he is slow in his intellectual skills. This may not be the case at all. Although he may appear to be slow in learning, it may only be because he is so physically involved that it takes him more time to perform intellectual skills than it does the average child.

If labels must be used, they should be used discriminately. The danger of mislabeling an individual can adversely affect his whole life. Feelings such as depression and a sense of worthlessness can engulf a disabled individual as a result of having a haphazard label placed on him. This was true in Bill's case.

When Bill came to my office for a college planning conference I noticed that he was quick to say, "I do not think I can do that." When I asked him why he said it so often, he told me that ever since he was seven years old he had been told in school that he was a dumb, special-ed kid. Thus, when Bill reached the age of eighteen and had graduated from high school, he still was reacting to the label that had been carelessly placed on him some years before. It took a lot of reassuring before Bill grasped the idea that he might not be as dumb as people had said he was.

After an extensive psychological evaluation, it was determined that Bill was college material. At first, thinking of himself as such was difficult. He had been conditioned to think he was dumb. When he did enter college, he had no trouble performing like any other student. Today he is a counselor in one of the country's big rehabilitation centers.

To stereotype a disabled person causes many problems. Rehabilitation experts are often guilty of using indiscriminate labels that can have a traumatic affect on a disabled individual. This was true in Todd's case. When the psychologist entered Todd's room at the rehabilitation hospital to conduct counseling sessions with him, the shades were drawn, the lights were out, and Todd lay huddled in his bed. When asked why he had resorted to such a state, he whispered that the doctor had just told him he would never walk again. "You are now one of the disabled population," the doctor bluntly informed Todd. This was devastating for him to hear.

"If I cannot walk, does that mean I am mentally retarded?" Todd wondered out loud. Somewhere he had gotten the impression that people thought those who could not walk were likewise mentally retarded. All Todd knew was that now he was going from being a successful junior executive to spending the rest of his life sitting in a wheelchair. Todd angrily blurted out, "How am I to make my living now? No one will hire me in this state. I have a family to support. What am I supposed to do?"

Todd could have been spared this emotional impact had the doctor taken the time to explain what life might be like from then on. Bluntly classifying him as a member of the so-called disabled population did not sit positively with Todd. He was not ready yet to attach such a classification to himself. Being forced to do so sent his psychological comfort levels plummeting.

The cases of Bill and Todd vividly point out the importance of using specific terminology when discussing a disability. Emotional trauma and agony can be prevented when the disabled individual is provided with specific wording concerning his condition. Had the school administrators in the case of Bill been up-front in their terminology of the boy, he would have not gone through so many years of mislabeling himself in his own mind. His parents also might have helped him in this respect had they been counseled to tell him, "Yes, you do not walk as well as other boys and you never will. You keep trying to do the best you can."

Todd may have benefited from the same direct confrontation with a family member or a therapist. It was not that the doctor was too blunt with him, but that he did not give Todd all the facts. This is one time when bluntness in conversation can be a good tool. Caution should be practiced in regard to the vocabulary used in such an instance. If the disabled person seems intellectually able to understand what is said to him, everything about his condition should be told. This may first cause him to be emotionally upset. Eventually, however, what he has been told can be of consolation.

When the disabled individual becomes a victim of wrong labeling, the negative affects on his future life are significant. Being labeled incorrectly once may result in being incorrectly labeled for the rest of one's life. Incorrect labeling does not realistically define disabled people in society. Parents, medical professionals, and rehabilitation personnel all have a responsibility to correctly identify and label individuals with physical deficiencies. Not to accept such a responsibility does the disabled individual an irrevocable disservice.

Should Disabled Children Be Disciplined?

Disciplining a disabled child is often frowned upon. Parents wonder if such a child should be disciplined. The answer is simple. Not only should he be disciplined, but he *must* be disciplined. A disability should not be used as an excuse for allowing a disabled child to misbehave.

Discipline helps all children develop self-control. The disabled child is no exception. Teaching him right from wrong, and the difference between doing what he wants to do and what he is asked to do is as important to his training as it is to any other child. Learning how to control his behavior is his first step toward becoming master of himself.

There are many methods for administering discipline. One approach is to sit the child on a chair or send him to his room. Either approach yields results. After a certain period of time, tell the child why he is being isolated from others. Urge him to think over what he did or said that was not acceptable. Discuss his misbehavior with him. Listen carefully to his reasoning. If it is necessary to discipline him a second time, be consistent in your approach.

A child with unintelligible speech may pose a more complicated disciplinary problem. Nevertheless, if he misbehaves, he should be disciplined. If he cannot speak and explain his behavior, he should be trained to raise his hand or blink his eyes to signal his negative or positive response to questions asked of him. For example, if he is asked, "Do you know why you did that?" He should be able to gesture yes or no. If he gestures yes, the next question can be, "Do you think you should be punished for doing that?" If he gestures no, ask him why not. Does he think he was a good boy? Or does he think he did do something wrong? Both questions require a yes or no answer.

When the disabled child feels that someone cares enough to listen to him, it gives him a sense of importance. Being accused of misbehaving and not being able to express why he did or he did not do a certain thing would be a frustrating experience for any child. Expressing himself in his own way develops positive feelings of self-worth. He lacks such feelings when people talk over his head to one another, not consulting him about anything.

The child who can discipline himself trusts himself. He is outgoing and self-assured. Although his disability may embarrass him, if he is well disciplined he learns to manage the embarrassment. He handles the disability's side effects well. In essence, regardless of his age, he is a child on the road to becoming adjusted to his disability.

The child who has never learned to discipline himself will exhibit immature behavior. If he feels like crying, he cries. If he has difficulty performing a skill, he may pick up an object and throw it across the room. If he becomes overwhelmed with frustration, he throws a temper tantrum. Such a child has not learned to control himself.

Twelve-year-old Melanie demonstrates how important self-discipline and self-control are. Because she was never disciplined at home, Melanie did not follow directions, did not do as she was asked, and did not interact with peers. When she was told to concentrate on the task she was doing, Melanie flew into a rage. She resented all authority. Everything she did and everything she said was on impulse. If at lunchtime no one helped her carry her tray, she dumped her food on the floor and lay down and kicked her feet. If she wanted a person's attention, she pinched the person. Melanie lacked respect for everyone. She also had no respect for herself. She had never learned how to be respectful at home. Therefore, she saw no reason to show respect to anyone outside the home.

To rehabilitate a child with Melanie's uncontrolled characteristics is a tremendous undertaking. Therapists and teachers had difficulty getting Melanie to cooperate. Suffice it to say, nothing can be accomplished with such a child until she can demonstrate self control. It is necessary for the child to be able to discipline herself if any therapeutic progress is to be made. Self-discipline is a major ingredient in such a process. The younger the age at the time it is introduced, the better it is for the child.

As unintentional as it may be, parents are being cruel to their disabled child when they do not insist that he exhibit acceptable behavior. As he grows older, he will get nowhere and make no progress if he has not learned to be in control of himself. This is often overlooked, not only by parents, but also by a surprising number of rehabilitation specialists. Rehabilitation, therapy, surgery, and medication are the only disciplines considered important. Although they are important to the child's progress, they do not supply all of the answers.

What the Law Says

It comes as news to many people, parents in particular, that there are United States Federal Laws pertaining to the education and welfare of the disabled child. Such laws are not usually brought to the attention of the very people who should be familiar with them. Listed below are parental rights pertaining to the child attending public school. Knowledge of them can do much to lessen feelings of uncertainty and hopelessness relating to the disabled child's plight.

- Parents have the right to participate in every decision related to the identification, evaluation, and placement of their child or youth with a disability.
- Parents must give consent for any initial evaluation, assessment, or placement; be notified of any change in placement that may occur; be included, along with teachers, in conferences and meetings held to draw up individualized programs; and must approve these plans before they go into effect for the first time.
- The right of parents to challenge and appeal any decision related to the identification, evaluation, and placement, or any issue concerning the provision of Free Appropriate Public Education, of their child is fully protected by clearly spelled out due process procedures.
- Parents have the right to confidentiality of information. No one may see a child's records unless the parents give their written permission. (The exception to this is school personnel with legitimate educational interests.)

P.L. 99–372, The Handicapped Children's Protection Act of 1986
This law was enacted in 1986 "to amend the Education of the Handicapped Act to authorize the award of reasonable attorneys' fees to certain prevailing parties, to clarify the effect of the Education of the Handicapped Act on rights, procedures, and remedies under the other laws relating to the prohibition of discrimination, and for other purposes." Public Law 99–372: provides for reasonable attorneys' fees and costs to parents and guardians who prevail in administrative hearings or court when there is a dispute with a school system concerning their child's right to a free appropriate special education and related services;

- applies to all cases initiated after July 3, 1984; and
- requests the General Accounting Office to study the impact of the law and submit findings to Congress concerning the number of com-

plaints, prevailing parties, amounts of attorneys' fees, and other data. [This study was completed in 1989. To receive a copy of the findings, call the U.S. General Accounting Office at (202) 512-6000 (V) or (301) 413-0006 (TTY) and ask for report GAO/HRD-90–22BR.]

P.L. 100–146, The Developmental Disabilities and Bill of Rights Act Amendments of 1987

The Act was amended in 1990 (P.L. 101–496) and in 1994 (P.L. 103–230) by the Developmental Disabilities Assistance and Bill of Rights Act of 1994. The formula grants to support Councils in the states are for promoting, through systemic change, capacity building, and advocacy activities, the development of a consumer and family centered, comprehensive system and a coordinated array of culturally competent services, supports, and other assistance designed to achieve independence, productivity, and integration and inclusion into the community. Another key provision of these amendments was the definition of "developmental disability," which means: severe, chronic disability of an individual five years of age or older that: (a) is attributable to a mental or physical impairment or combination of mental and physical impairments; (b) is manifested before the person attains age twenty-two; (c) is likely to continue indefinitely; (d) results in substantial functional limitations in three or more of the following areas of major life activity: (i) self-care; (ii) receptive and expressive language; (iii) learning; (iv) mobility; (v) self-direction; (vi) capacity for independent living; and (vii) economic sufficiency; and (e) reflects the individual's need for a combination and sequence of special, interdisciplinary, or generic services, supports, or other assistance that is of lifelong or extended duration and is individually planned and coordinated.

CHAPTER 3

Challenges the Teenager Faces

Teenage years are filled with challenges. Problems unexpectedly pop up in every teenager's life. A good friend down the street decides he does not want to be a good friend any longer. Homework gobbles up too much time. There is no time left for doing fun things. Looking forward to dating is a major step in maturity.

The disabled teenager experiences the same situations. He is as sensitive to his environment and those in it as any other teenager. There is one difference, however. His problems are more intense. The teen years are precarious years for him. During this time in his development he becomes acutely aware of his disability. All at once he realizes how it prevents him from taking up the same activities as every other teenager.

Like every teenager, the disabled teenager matures. His problem at this time is trying to impress his maturity on those around him. If he is confined to a wheelchair, or is isolated in his home, his experiences in life will be limited. This can be why his maturity does not develop as readily as that of the nondisabled teenager. When he compares himself with other teenagers, he is conscious of the differences in his development.

The disabled teenager easily conjures up a negative concept of himself. Often he cannot help doing this. Society significantly influences his development. Few people take the time to understand why this is true. They do not consider such questions as: What affect does society's attitudes have on him? Does he worry about how he is judged? How does he feel when people stare at him? Now, ask yourself these questions: How do you feel in the presence of a disabled young person? Do you play any part in his developing a poor concept of himself? Do you feel that there is a real person under the physical disability? Honest answers to these questions expose society's attitudes toward the disabled.

Interaction between the disabled and nondisabled teenager should take place. However, it often does not. Whether or not it takes place depends upon the answers to some revealing questions. How well is the teenager adjusted to his disability? How social is he? Does he easily greet strangers? Even though he may not be able to speak clearly or get about by himself, he should still make the attempt to interact with his peers. If he possesses the intellect to think, then he possesses the intellect to associate with those around him.

The physically disabled teenager who sits and stares blankly into space gives a false impression of his capabilities. It is not necessary to be able to walk, speak intelligibly, or dress and feed oneself to possess a congenial attitude. A smile from the disabled teenager, an effort to shake hands, or just voicing "hi" is sufficient. Any of these gestures convey positive feelings toward another person. He will portray the opposite should he frown, have a blank stare, or cry or laugh uncontrollably.

Parents play a significant role in shaping their teenager's conduct outside the home. If he is not required to exhibit mature behavior in the home, his emotional and intellectual development will likely be significantly below his chronological age level. For example, if he is fourteen or fifteen years old, but behaves like a five-year-old, he is emotionally functioning below his birth age.

A Good Self-Concept Is Important

Everyone needs to develop a healthy concept of himself. This is easier said than done. Some people have no trouble creating a good picture of themselves in their minds. Other people have difficulty doing so and never succeed. The disabled teenager is such a person.

Although every teenager must cope with negative feelings about themselves, these feelings are more pronounced in the disabled teenager. For instance, it is essential that he not develop feelings of self-rejection and self-hate. His disability constantly reminds him that it can embarrass him any time, any place. He cannot be sure how his disability will cause him to behave. For example, when looking for books in the public library, he cannot be certain that he will not tear the pages in a book. He thinks of how embarrassing it could be if he were to drop the book in the quietness of the library. He knows everyone would look at him. Feelings of anticipation penetrate his thinking every minute. He is always expecting the worst to happen.

Shielding himself with a sense of positiveness can help the teenager come to terms with the daily embarrassments his disability can impose. *One point he must learn is that it is not always the public who looks down on him, but he who looks down on himself.* It is important that he not judge himself too severely. He will feel more comfortable if he can bring himself to accept what he can do well and adjust to what he cannot do.

Society is pretty well tuned in to how the disabled teenager regards himself. If he has a good concept of himself and gives the impression that he does like himself, people will readily interact with him. How he regards himself will determine how they regard him. All the chips for success are in his hands. It is up to the disabled teenager to play them accordingly.

The teenager who has a good opinion of himself will have little trouble developing a sense of independence. If he is in a wheelchair, he still can be independent. If he cannot express himself orally, he may exhibit a desire for independence through body behavior or facial expressions. For instance, while sitting in a crowded room he can project a sense of independence by not interrupting the conversations of others. This means that no one has to be attentive to him. A disability is not a legitimate excuse for being dependent on others. Although the teenager may not be able to be physically independent he can, in all probability, be intellectually, emotionally, and socially independent. If he has the desire he can exhibit some form of independence.

How Parental Attitudes Influence Teenagers

Every teenager is a product of his home environment. It has a deciding affect on his life. The type of discipline the parents administer to the disabled teenager, the attitudes they express toward him, and the tone of voice they use with him, all have an influence on the way he interacts with people. The same approaches affect how the teenager adjusts to his disability.

Unexpected problems occur if the disabled teenager is overprotected. Although this is an abnormal situation in the rearing of nondisabled teenagers, it is a normal occurrence in the rearing of a disabled teenager.

There are many ways to be too overprotective. It does not only mean being too physically overprotective but can also mean being too overprotective of the teenager's mind. For instance, the sixteen year old disabled teenager should not be protected against knowing how heartbreaking it is to his parents that he is disabled. Although he should not feel he must apologize for being disabled, he should make the effort to understand his parents' turmoil. This makes it possible for him to lessen noticeably the emotional impact his disability causes them.

Being overprotective of any child can cause him to be self centered, demanding of others' attention, and frightened to interact with strangers. Overprotectiveness can encase a child in his own problems. It allows no freedom for the development of self-initiative or self-exertion. The child becomes impassive to everything around him. He will find it frightening and disconcerting to function in any manner without his parents.

What Is a Thin-Line Disability?

While the disability of many teenagers is obvious to the naked eye, there are disabilities that are barely obvious. These are defined as *thin-line disabilities*. In the minds of the public, such a teenager is neither disabled nor nondisabled. For the family and the teenager himself, this status can cause many problems and feelings of uncertainty. The teenager does not know how to classify himself. Therefore, he prefers to think of himself as nondisabled. Many times the parents follow suit. If the deficiency is not noticeable, it is easy for them to think of their offspring as nondisabled.

With the many normal problems that all teenagers have to cope with, having a physical condition that is practically undefinable makes life more complex. How a teenager's disability is medically classified may be questionable. If one foot slightly drags when he walks, one hand is minus five fingers, or he has a minor quiver in his coordination ability, these characteristics determine the teenager's medical classification. The fact that, in spite of these characteristics, he may physically perform as well as any other teenager adds to his uncertain classification. "He just has a little shaking in the hands, that's all. He does everything we can do," neighborhood kids remark. Just as long as the teenager keeps up with them, his peers see nothing wrong with him.

It is a very different story when the doctor is consulted. Even though there are no visible signs of being disabled in any way, it is a jolting experience for the teenager to be classified as disabled. Undoubtedly until now, the teenager considered himself nondisabled. Although he knew he had a minor physical problem, as long as it did not interfere with what he wanted to do, he could easily put it out of his mind.

A teenager with a thin-line disability can become a victim of many psychological problems. Feeling that he must, in some way, hide his physical deficiency from peers, is one of these problems. When he feels he must hide his deficiency there is also a temptation to deny the whole matter. He feels compelled to hide it.

When a teenager with a thin-line disability juggles his concept of himself between being disabled and nondisabled, other psychological problems arise. He can only do such juggling for a certain period of time. Eventually he will become tired of trying to fool himself into thinking nothing is wrong. He may resort to daydreaming or fantasizing. Invariably the teenager will come across people who will notice his physical problem. If they ask him about it, his reaction undoubtedly will be one of anger, denial, or disgust.

Suggesting to the teenager that he face the truth takes unusual patience. Few fourteen, sixteen, and eighteen year olds want to admit to any flaws in themselves. When they have to, it can be devastating. Unless sensitivity is practiced in counseling such a teenager, his psychological comfort levels plummet very quickly. On the other hand, if counseled to recognize the extent of his physical problem the teenager will be spared a great deal of psychological turmoil. When the teenager can recognize and adjust to the fact that he does have problems, he will find associating with others much easier.

Adjusting to a Disability

The physically disabled teenager is normal in some ways and abnormal in others. This is difficult for people to understand. They have difficulty accepting a person or object that deviates from what is considered normal. The basic truth is that the disabled teenager's attitudes and presentations of himself are what will determine how people will judge him. If he handles his disability with poise and dignity, people will react positively to him. If he behaves otherwise, they will negatively react to him.

While a seven year old child seemingly takes his physical limitations in stride, this is not as easy for the sixteen or seventeen year old. His reaction to worry matures as he matures. For example, his biggest worry is how his disability will affect his social standing with friends. Will they invite him to parties or will they ignore him? How will girls feel about him? Will they want to date him or, will they find an excuse for not accepting his invitation?

Sixteen-year-old Ellen had to deal with such questions. She wondered if boys would date her since she had an artificial leg. She soon discovered her dating would be limited. Although the boys hung out with Ellen and obviously liked her, they never asked her out on a date. They were worried what friends might think if they dated her. Peers can be some of the harshest critics for teenagers to cope with.

There is no way Ellen, or anyone else, can rectify this situation. Developing relationships with boys can be is a heartbreaking experience. Such incidences do occur in the disabled teenage girl's life and must be faced. The kindest thing to do is to allow the girl to go through a grieving period about it, adjust to it, and then go on with her life. Teenagers discriminate between what is acceptable to them and what is not. Before he does anything that might reflect on him, he looks about to see who is watching. He worries about how his friends might judge him.

Physically disabled teenagers must adjust to what is acceptable to society and what is not. For example, a nondisabled boy dating a disabled girl is generally not accepted. If a relationship does develop, however, and after dating the girl over a period of time, the boy all at once senses criticism from his peers, he will drop the girl quickly. Being dumped by a boy can be more emotionally upsetting to a girl than it was for her to realize that dating boys was not likely to be a part of her life. Having a taste of what it is like and then having it quickly withdrawn is far more painful.

The disabled boy can experience the same type of rejection. Many girls do not like to date disabled boys. A nondisabled girl may be more blunt in her rejection or refusal to accept an invitation from a disabled boy. Such rejection becomes an automatic part of the disabled boy's life. His alternative also is to adjust. It is essential that both the girls and boys try not to reject themselves.

A teenager who has adjusted well to his disability realistically views his future life. Although he should certainly not avoid making plans for his future, they should be realistic plans. If it is obvious he will never walk by himself, plans to go hunting when he is older should never be considered. The same applies to a girl. If she cannot walk, attending the high school prom and dancing with all the good-looking boys is not likely. Hard as it may be for the physically disabled teenager, it is important to take stock of one's physical abilities and inabilities, and behave accordingly. To entertain any other type of reasoning invariably results in heart-ache, disbelief, and a continual state of depression and unhappiness.

Fears Common to Most Disabled Teenagers

Teenage years are a critical time for the young disabled person. He is critical of himself and others. He may be just learning that because of the disability, he will do things slower than his friends. One of his greatest fears is that his slowness and inability to do things will cause others not to like him. He does not yet understand the implications of his disability.

Fear of being rejected by peers is powerful. So powerful that it can push the disabled teenager beyond his capacities. When these fears go unresolved, or become exaggerated, they can become coupled with hate and linked with destructive feelings such as jealousy and envy. At this stage the teenager needs to form a firm foundation on which to build his life. He needs to be reassured many times over that other people like him for what he is and not for the way he may walk or talk. Any other approach fails to feed growth and development. Below is a table of the most common fears and the reasons for them developing during the teenage years.

Fears Common to Some Disabled Teenagers

Fear	Reasons for Carrying Over into Teenage Levels
Fear of loud noises, such as thunder, slamming doors, and other auditory sounds.	Particular brain injury may cause spasmodic reaction to loud noises; teenager may fear his inability to protect himself from harm at this time.
Spatial: bed or other furniture moved from usual place, moving to new environment, e.g. home, school, etc.	May fear falling out of bed, fears not being accepted in new surroundings and by those in them.
Mother or father going out at night.	May fear being rejected; fears loss of parents; worries about who will care

	for him should the parent not return.
Concrete, down-to-earth fears, bodily harm, falling.	Conscious of feelings of insecurity; may be aware of physical inability to protect himself at certain times.
Fear of one or both parents' death.	Fears being left permanently with strangers; concern over possibility of having no one who cares about him often fears he will be placed in some kind of institution.
Fear of being lost.	Senses inability to get around by himself and keep up with others; fears being left behind in a lonely place and unable to find goal by himself.
Fear of sleeping alone in a room or of being only one on floor of house.	Due to infantile fear of the dark, may feel constant need for parental physical presence because of acute feelings of insecurity.
Worries about things: not being liked, being late for school and other appointment.	Finds handicap a serious, hindrance; conscious that speech or walk may be different from others; aware of the attitudes of others toward him.
No one will marry me.	Marriage being a normal process in any man or woman's life, the prospect that his handicap may keep a teenager from marriage can be a source of fear to him. He may look toward marriage as a means of legal companionship when his parents die, as a chance to prove to himself and others that, handicap or not, he can produce children, or it can be a means for satisfying normal sexual drives. The chances that normal sex life may not be allowed to some handicapped teenagers may prey on

his mind—if not consciously, then unconsciously.

No one will give me a job.

Being self-supporting and able to buy what he wants when he wants it is important to every teenager and young adult. The prospect that a handicap may make it difficult, if not impossible, for him to earn money and be financially independent creates many fears. "How will I buy food, pay rent, and buy clothes?" is a basic concern to the teenager or young adult. In his mind, his very ability to exist as a human being is in jeopardy because of his physical disability. Furthermore, the desire to buy for others—and, by so doing, show his love or win their concern and respect for himself—can also make him uncertain.

Feelings of personal inadequacy.

Not being able to compete with the abilities of brothers or sisters can be a source of fear to the teenager with a handicap. He feels threatened; his place in the family becomes uncertain. His image in the eyes of his parents, as well as others, can suffer and cause fear that he will not measure up.

Disabled Sibling vs. Nondisabled Sibling

When two teenagers, one of whom is disabled, live in the same home, many adjustments must be made. It is quite normal that as the teenagers mature, each evaluates the other. This becomes even more profound as the disabled teenager becomes aware that his brother or sister can do more than he can. The nondisabled teenager also has a problem that he must work out. His disabled sibling can be embarrassing to him. Friends ask questions, and when they are invited over to his house, they may find a reason for not coming. Parental guidance is definitely needed at this time.

A variety of problems can pepper the relationship between the two teenagers. The type of problems are determined by the siblings' ages. If the disabled teenager is two years older and cannot perform the same activities as his younger sibling it can be an upsetting situation. He resents the fact that his able brother or sister can bypass him in abilities. On the other side, the nondisabled sibling may revel in the fact that he can do activities better than his older disabled sister or brother. This rivalry is normal.

Much of the dissension between two siblings can be contributed to a lack of understanding. This will occur when time is not taken to explain to the nondisabled teenager his sibling's disability. He undoubtedly has many questions needing answers. He might be entertaining the fear that he may become disabled. He might wonder whether his disabled sibling will ever be able to perform certain skills. These questions will daily penetrate the nondisabled sibling's mind. Answers should have been given to him when he was younger. But before any answers can be given, parents must be able to handle their own feelings. This will avoid any chance of imparting negative information or emotions to the nondisabled sibling.

Tensions can be minimized if both teenagers are included in the conversation describing the disability. It can be a good learning experience. They can exchange information with each other about the disability and share feelings.

Sometimes parents find it difficult to divide their time evenly between two teenagers. Yet, fairness is important to avoid damaging one or the other. For example, overindulging the nondisabled sibling can result in damaging his personality. This happens when parents see nothing wrong with expressing to the nondisabled sibling their frustration and dissatisfaction with the physically disabled sibling.

One father pointed out to his disabled daughter how lucky she was to have a sister who did not mind playing with her. He emphasized how embarrassing she was to her sister. If the neighborhood kids wanted to go to the drugstore for a cold drink, and they invited the disabled sibling to go along, she was to refuse to go. She was to let her sister go without having to worry about helping her disabled sibling drink a cola or eat an ice cream cone. The nondisabled sibling got the impression from her father that she was an extra-special person when compared to her disabled sister.

Parents work against themselves when they allow the intensity of depression, grief, and disappointment to influence their judgement. An emotionally distraught parent can result in an emotionally distraught child. Pitting a nondisabled child against his sibling can result in psychological turmoil. More is gained when parents interweave the disabled child and his special needs into the family circle. Although this is not easy, it can be done.

There is nothing wrong in requiring the nondisabled sibling to assist in the care of his disabled sibling. To what extent should be determined by the age of each sibling. For example, if the disabled sibling is eight years old and his nondisabled sibling is five years old, expecting the five year old to do much is ludicrous. However, when the disabled sibling becomes eleven or twelve years old and the nondisabled sibling reaches the ages of nine or ten, initial training of how he can assist should begin. It is important that the nondisabled sibling not be overburdened with the care of the disabled sibling.

Working out a schedule when the nondisabled sibling is available to help with the care of his disabled sibling is wise. For instance, during vacation from school, a half-hour or an hour per morning might be set aside when the two siblings would engage in a mutual activity. This can be a good time for the nondisabled sibling to teach his disabled sibling rules to a game, or how to do a specific activity. If he is old enough, the brother or sister might be paid to baby-sit the disabled sibling when the parents go out for an evening.

Important Personality Traits

The personality of the disabled teenager is complex. Few professionals stop to think about the affect a disability can have on a teenager. Those treating the teenager are sometimes so occupied in helping him overcome the problems his disability presents that they neglect how his personality might be affected. Before these assets can be developed they must be identified and defined. The following chart lists the positive and negative traits that can make up a disabled teenager's personality.

Important Personality Traits

Trait	*Definition*
Self-acceptance.	An attitude toward oneself and one's personal qualities that are of unique worth to one. One has an unemotional recognition of one's ability and limitations, one's virtues

	and faults, without feeling unnecessarily guilty or blaming oneself for that which one cannot help.
Self-actualization.	The process of developing capacities and certain talents, of understanding and accepting oneself, of integrating one's motives.
Self-assertion.	An ability in social situations to strive for achievement of realistic goals; also, in certain cases, the ability to develop a certain sense of leadership in a group.
Self-consistency.	Behavior that shows itself in high conformity with a common pattern of behavior that is determined by a given situation as well as long-term goals; the development of a picture of self and the progressively greater harmonizing of behavior with the environment around oneself.
Self-criticism.	A recognition of behavior patterns that do not conform to those others have adopted; the ability to recognize realistically one's own strengths and weaknesses.
Self-determination.	An ability to regulate behavior, not just by immediate circumstances nor by direct social pleasures, but by personal initiative and for the sake of attaining goals in life.
Self-realization.	An ability to balance and harmonize some development of all aspects in one's personality and to develop personal potentialities that one is capable of doing.
Self-regard.	The sentiment of one who seeks to enhance oneself and to develop a

feeling of satisfaction when a situation (physical, social, or emotional) can be favorable.

Self-system.	A final choice of potentialities that one seeks to develop and to integrate into one's personality. Not all these tendencies are consciously recognized, and most may be rejective alternatives that are repressed rather than brought to the conscious level of thinking and reasoning.

Undesirable Personality Traits

Trait	*Definition*
Aggression.	He may display hostile behavior, behavior that causes fear, and which can bring him into forceful contact with other people around him. It often is connected with feelings of frustration and the teenager's need to prove himself at all costs. He may express it against a person or object that is causing him to have feelings of frustration. By so doing, he hopes to overcome the frustration and to be able to control the person or handle the object as a non-handicapped boy or girl his age would.
Anxiety.	He may have a present or continuing strong desire or drive that misses its goal. This condition is a state of continual fear, either strong or low in anxiety. Feelings of being threatened may also accompany it.
Depression.	He usually will not respond to any kind of stimulation and has a lowered initiative. He very often has

gloomy thoughts. He may be restless, have periods of despair, and have a tendency to self-condemn himself.

Guilt.

He may have a feeling of regretfulness for something he thinks he has or has not done. Guilt is often accompanied by indirect expressions and a poor sense of personal worth. Sometimes it can be imagined guilt that may be deeply repressed. Parents' attitudes very often can be a contributing factor.

Self-abasement.

He is often very submissive and has strong feelings of inferiority. He yields to other people. This trait is often related to the degree of his handicap.

Self-abuse.

He misunderstands both his handicapped self and his real self, which often results in excessive masturbation and self-degradation.

Self-accusation.

He blames himself, usually falsely, and to a serious degree. This often is connected closely with how he regards himself and how his handicap, major or minor, limits him in living a normal life.

Self-deception.

He fails to recognize the realistic aspects of his situation and some things that closely concern him.

Self-extinction.

He has little sense of his own personality as a self-experiencing, self-directing entity. Very often he will try to live through the lives of those in his immediate environment, seeing himself only as a reflection of them.

Understanding Masculinity and Femininity

The way people talk to the disabled teenager has an affect on how feminine and masculine traits are developed. If people are condescending, the teenager will respond accordingly. If they address him appropriately for his age, he will measure up to their expectations. Answering a request from either a boy or girl by saying, "I will get it for you, just a minute. Just as soon as I am through doing this," imparts to the teenager that he must wait his turn like everyone else. Addressing him in this manner shows him respect.

Nineteen-year-old Jake was lucky. To enhance his sense of masculinity his father took him to the neighborhood bar. This gave Jake an opportunity to rub shoulders with other males. Here he could become familiar with "male talk." After several such visits, Jake's sense of importance soared. His masculine traits started to develop. He grew a beard (even though someone had to keep it in good shape for him) and he insisted that he be present when it was time to buy new clothes. Jake had very definite ideas of what he wanted to wear. The clothes were all the latest styles. They also emulated what was worn around Jake at the bar. His boyhood took flight and was replaced with maturity.

Chapter 8 provides a list of personal "tools" that can make life easier for both the disabled teenage boy and girl. These everyday "tools" can give them independence, at least partially. Addresses of the companies that provide many of the products are listed as well.

Mixing Femininity with a Disability

The stigma that society attaches to a disability has a traumatic affect on the disabled individual. Disabled teenage girls are particularly affected. They are no different from any other girl. They all strive to appear feminine. This striving is not an easy undertaking. The disabled girl has to work extra hard toward developing her femininity. She, more than the average girl, benefits from being introduced to feminine things. When she is, she will feel lovely, look lovely, and take pride in herself.

A mother can have a positive affect on her teenage daughter. There are many ways she can do this. For instance, helping her to comb her hair is a good time to tell her that she is attractive and has such pretty hair. When the daughter hears this it encourages her to think positively about herself. For a mother to show her disabled daughter how to apply makeup can also be helpful. Learning to do this is important to every teenager. It is an important way to emphasize their attractiveness. Yet, such attractiveness can be spoiled if too much makeup is applied. Learning to add to natural attractiveness rather than detract from it with too much makeup is an important step for every teenage girl to make. The physically disabled girl must realize that putting on too much makeup can detract from her appearance and also draw attention to her disability.

Some parents feel the need to shield their teenager from doing what other teenagers do. This was true of sixteen year old Amy. Although she was confined to a wheelchair and was a sophomore in high school, her mother was fiercely afraid that some boy would take advantage of her. She based her fears on the fact that Amy was attractive, very verbal in discussion with classmates, and yearned to be a member of their social circle.

Amy's mother complained to everyone how much trouble it was to get Amy ready for school. When it was asked if Amy might wear lipstick and earrings, her mother rebelled. "Don't you think I have enough to do every morning just getting her dressed? There is no extra time to put makeup and earrings on her." Amy's yearnings made no difference to her mother.

The day Amy came to school with lipstick and earrings on she was happy as a lark. "How do I look? Do you think the boys will like me now?" she asked. There was one flaw in all this. Amy had no idea which pair of earrings she was wearing. Being pressed for time that morning, her mother had not allowed Amy to look in the mirror. When she was told how pretty her earrings were she asked, "What color are they? Are they the round ones?"

The fact that Amy wanted to wear makeup that day also irritated her mother. Putting the makeup on Amy was one more thing she had to do that morning. After she had gone to school, her mother lost no time calling the principal and telling him to make sure that the boys did not take sexual advantage of Amy. "This is one reason why I did not want her to start to wear makeup," she said. It was hard to persuade the mother that Amy's request to wear earrings and makeup was a normal teenage request. That her daughter might be normal in some respect never occurred to her mother.

A delicate area where femininity should be practiced is the monthly menstruation period. For some girls this time of the month can be a chore. Others are able to handle it well. Impressing the importance of cleanliness at this time is essential. Failure of the physically disabled girl to make sure she is clean at this time can detract from her femininity.

For teenage girls who have not been educated to the facts of life, the menstrual period can be frightening. All at once, they discover they are bleeding and do not know why. More times than not, parents assume that because their daughter is disabled, there is no reason to tell her about the changes that take place in her body. Parents of disabled girls frequently assume that these changes do not occur. Nothing could be further from the truth. Like any other girl in her teenage years, the disabled girl goes through hormonal changes.

Carrie is a case in point. At age sixteen she had begun to menstruate. However, no one had ever prepared her for this event. It was only after the author treated her for unexplained depression that it was discovered she had started to menstruate and feared doing so. In a counseling session she was eventually able to admit that she was scared that she was going to bleed to death. She wanted to know how it could be stopped or if she should go to the doctor. When asked if she had told her mother, Carrie said she had but was told not to worry about it.

Once Carrie understood the process of menstruation, her fear of bleeding to death subsided. The twenty-eight day cycle was explained and how important it would be for Carrie to keep track on a calendar when she would menstruate again. Being encouraged to take personal control of her body did much for Carrie's self-concept. The boost in her self-concept also helped her to build self-esteem. She began to think of herself as an important person.

The menstrual period is a good time to emphasize femininity to the physically disabled teenage girl. The introduction of magazines acclaiming the femininity of a teenager is also helpful. Like any other, the disabled teenager can enjoy looking at the pictures and dreaming about what it would be like to wear that bathing suit, those pair of shorts, or that dress. It can point out to her that taking such immaculate care of herself, while it cannot eradicate the disability, it can take her a long way toward de-emphasizing it.

Mixing Masculinity with a Disability

The masculine aspect of a disabled male teenager's makeup is at stake as he grows older. Too often his parents do not prepare him for the noticeable physical changes that will occur. He may be just realizing at the age of fourteen what it means to be a male. Even though he may be of average intelligence, if he was not exposed to the environment around him, his intellectual, emotional, and social interest may still be at the eight or nine year old level. He may never have had any association with boys his own age.

The male teenager may become obsessed with impressing on those around him that he is no longer a little boy, but is a young man. However, this reclassification is not easily recognized by people in society. The male teenager, himself, is the only person who can justify the reclassification. No one else knows how to do it for him.

A major obstacle occurs when the male disabled teenager is totally dependent upon his family. It can become a serious problem if he is totally dependent upon his mother for care. There is a difference in a male helping another male compared to a female taking care of a male. One danger is that the development of the male ego can easily be impaired. This is not as likely to happen when there is a male role model in the home. Such a role model can easily point out to the disabled teenager necessary masculine traits. Just because the teenager has a disability is no reason for him to be stripped of his masculinity.

The Disabled Teenager's Sexuality

Of the many elements that make up every human being, the element of sexuality is rarely affected. Every human being is a sexual being. The physically disabled teenager is no different. He has sex drives just like any other teenager. Regardless of the severity of his disability, his sexuality is rarely disabled. Out of control, needing guidelines, yes. However, just as in other areas of development, he may have to face problems. His sexuality can be a significant problem to him. He has trouble thinking of himself as a physical and emotional person.

Physical and emotional changes occur within the disabled teenager just as within the average teenager. Sometimes these changes cause self degradation or be the source of feelings of frustration and anxiety. If the teenager has had no sex education as a young child, he may have difficulty exhibiting control of his drives at the ages of fourteen, sixteen, and eighteen. He may think nothing of satisfying his sexual feelings in public or in school. His urges may become so powerful that they take over his reasoning ability. When the teenager becomes comfortable with his sexuality he will not have the need to sexually act out to prove himself. He becomes aware of his sexual gender, his body changes, and his own reactions to certain stimulants. The teenager will no longer feel the need to prove to other people that there is something normal about him.

What the Law Says

Like everything else in society, Laws cover different aspects of being disabled. Too frequently the disabled and those determining their future are not familiar with these Laws. Few know that there are any Laws at all.

Below is the United States Law as it applies to those addressed in this Chapter. For some it may explain many irregularities that they have wondered about for some time. For others, becoming familiar with the Law helps to better serve the disabled individual. For those who wish to research the Law further, contact:

National Information Center for Children and Youth with Disabilities
P.O. Box 1492
Washington, DC 20013-1492
1-800-695-0285 Voice
E-mail: nichcy@aed.org
Website: www.nichcy.org

The *"Individual Disability Educational Act"* has been amended once since the amendment passed in 1990. The newest amendment, P.L. 102–119, primarily addressed the Part H program, now known as the Early Intervention Program for Infants and Toddlers with Disabilities.

The IDEA makes it possible for states and localities to receive federal funds to assist in the education of infants, toddlers, preschoolers, children, and youth with disabilities. Basically, in order to remain eligible for federal funds under the law, states must ensure that:

- All children and youth with disabilities, regardless of the severity of their disability, will receive a Free Appropriate Public Education (FAPE)—at public expense.
- Education of children and youth with disabilities will be based on a complete and individual evaluation and assessment of the specific, unique needs of each child.

- An Individualized Education Program (IEP), or an Individualized Family Services Plan (IFSP), will be drawn up for every child or youth found eligible for special education or early intervention services, stating precisely what kinds of special education and related services, or the types of early intervention services, each infant, toddler, preschooler, child, or youth will receive.
- To the maximum extent appropriate, all children and youth with disabilities will be educated in the regular education environment.
- Children and youth receiving special education have the right to receive the related services necessary to benefit from special education instruction. Related services include: . . . transportation and such developmental, corrective, and other supportive services as are required to assist a child with a disability to benefit from special education, and includes speech pathology and audiology, psychological services, physical and occupational therapy, recreation, including therapeutic recreation, early identification and assessment of disabilities in children, counseling services, including rehabilitation counseling, and medical services for diagnostic or evaluation purposes. The term also includes school health services, social work services in schools, and parent counseling and training (C.F.R.: Title 34; Education; Part 300.16, 1993).

CHAPTER 4

Challenges the Adult Faces

Everyone has to find a niche in society. Everyone has to seek out where he belongs. It can be one place for one person, another place for another person. This is a different experience for each and is just as true in the case of the disabled individual. He also must discover where he can fit in society. The difference here is that he is confronted with more complicated problems to solve. To make it even more difficult for him, many times there are no solutions to his problems. Nevertheless, he must honestly evaluate the problems as they apply to him. He must be knowledgeable as to their source and adjust to them.

The disabled individual must also evaluate his status as a disabled person. It is not easy for anyone to evaluate himself critically. It requires that he ask himself many questions: What are the positive aspects of my disability? Are there any? What are the negative aspects? Will my disability prevent me from taking care of myself? Will I find a job? Will I be able to live on my own? These questions must be candidly answered by the disabled individual. Only he knows how it feels to be disabled. The phrase: "It takes one to know one," has explicit meaning in this instance.

If the disabled adult is to become a social human being, it is important that he integrate himself into society. He cannot do this by attempting to impress others by behaving as if he were nondisabled. This places him under pressure. Few disabilities respond under pressure. Their characteristics become more pronounced. For example, even though he has poor coordination in his hands, the individual may still make the effort to pick up a cup of hot coffee. Rather than impress others that he is as normal as they are, he defeats his purpose. His hands are so poorly coordinated that the coffee spills down the front of him and all over the table. He does not realize he is exhibiting a lack of adjustment to his disability and embarrassing people around him. Drinking the coffee through a straw is far more acceptable.

If the disabled individual is to be a social being he must have the opportunity to interact with all types of people. Rubbing shoulders with others gives him an opportunity to become conditioned to the positive and negative reactions society may show him.

It is imperative that the physically disabled adult learn to adjust to society's attitudes and how those attitudes affect people differently. This can be difficult for the individual to understand if as a youth he was never brought directly into contact with his environment. This can result in his only knowing how to accept the attitudes and opinions of those closest to him. He never learned to form his own opinions.

Combining a Disability with Adulthood

The physically disabled adult develops an honest concept of himself by answering two questions: "What the does the world owe me?" and, "What do I owe the world?"

The answer to the first question is the world owes the physically disabled adult absolutely nothing. It is presumptuous of him to think it does. As for the second question, like any other person, the physically disabled person owes the world as much as he can give it. Perhaps he cannot give as much or as fast as other people, but he should be satisfied with what he can give. It is not what one gives to the world that counts, but if he gives it sincerely from within his soul.

The disabled person must find special ways to contribute to the world. If the individual thinks that because he is disabled he does not have to make any kind of contribution to society, he will not become a worthwhile person. He must accept the responsibility of giving to society as much as he can. When he accepts that responsibility with purpose, society will become aware that the disabled person can reach a high degree of normalcy.

John had trouble interweaving his disability into adulthood. His parents did not make it easy for him. They could not bring themselves to accept John as a typical young man. They regarded him as a disabled person only. One reason is that for many years they dressed him, fed him, and toileted him every day. Even when John reached the age of nineteen, his parents still saw him as a little boy. They continued to care for him as if he were an infant.

When John entered counseling, one of the first questions he wondered was why his parents treated him like a baby. It was explained to him that his parents had cared for him for nineteen years like an infant, which made it difficult for them to all at once accept him as an adult. He was told that if he did not want his parents to continue treating him like a little boy he must become director of his own life. If he did not take this step in maturity, he was told, he would be forced to remain under his parents' influence.

Stepping from the "Disabled World" into the Real World

Regardless of the severity of a disability, the physically disabled adult must develop a sense of importance. This requirement is paramount if he is to become productive in life. The way he makes this adjustment can negatively or positively affect his total development.

Many disabled individuals kid themselves into thinking they are making a positive social adjustment by associating only with people who are disabled like themselves. This is not the case. It does not enhance their intellectual or social development. One drawback is that the individual isolates himself from society by interacting with nonthreatening people like himself.

Entering the world of the nondisabled can be a nerve shattering experience. Leaving the protective surroundings of one's family and entering society's unprotective environment can be terrifying. This new environment is peppered with fears, apprehensions, and emotionally wrenching events. Necessary adjustments can make this easier for the disabled individual. He needs to learn how to interweave the positive attitudes of the nondisabled world into his "disabled" world.

When the physically disabled individual is satisfied by only congregating with other disabled persons like himself, he risks becoming contaminated by their negative attitudes. It is not recommended that persons with problems closely mingle with others who have the same problem. When they do, opportunities for physical, social, and intellectual advancement cannot take place.

Associating with people disabled like oneself leaves little margin for growth. There needs to be a margin for growth if the physically disabled individual wants to be treated like an adult. *Webster's Third New International Dictionary* defines "adulthood," as it applies to the nondisabled, in words and phrases such as independence, self-caring, and the ability to support oneself financially. When society looks at a disabled individual, its definition of adulthood is somewhat different. It defines the individual as one who requires care, has difficulty getting a job, and depends upon others for survival. Although this may be true in some cases, it does not apply to every disabled adult. Many are capable of fulfilling the adulthood definition as it applies to the nondisabled individual.

Peter is a case in point. He might not have been a vocational success had it not been for understanding friends who believed in his ability to succeed. Although he was mentally, socially, and emotionally ready to accept a job, he lacked the finances to go in search of one. Like any other young man in search of his first job, Peter needed financial backing. However, his family ignored this fact. No one had explained to them that most disabled individuals need "parental support services." Financial assistance, encouraging comments, and expressions of belief in the individual's capabilities can be reassuring to the young disabled individual. Peter's parents did not see it this way. They could not envision Peter supporting himself.

Fortunately, Peter's friends had a different opinion. They helped him out financially. Their expressions of faith in his ability made Peter's feelings of worth soar. They had the same faith in Peter that he had in himself. The confidence they expressed toward him could never be matched with any other source of support. Their unrelenting faith in Peter's ability helped him secure the job of his dreams. The job's salary allowed Peter to repay his friends.

It would have been incorrect for Peter to have taken his friends kindness as a matter of fact. For Peter not to have reimbursed them for the money they loaned him would have been inexcusable. Having a disability is no reason to take assistance for granted.

Being Director of One's Own Life

The disabled adult, who is of sound mind, should be allowed to be the director of his personal affairs. No one else should do this for him. A disability is no reason for an individual not to open his own mail, know how much money he has in the bank, or be consulted on purchasing his clothes. If he receives a monthly disability check, and cannot open it himself, it should not be opened for him. He has every right to have it opened in his presence. It should be considered his business, and no one else's. A disability should not be thought of as an element that can strip an individual of his rights to dignity and privacy.

Psychological problems are reduced when the disabled adult is director of his own life. Being able to decide for oneself what does or does not happen, can motivate an individual to great heights. To have someone else handle your affairs can be demoralizing. It can cause the individual to feel as if he is a second-class citizen.

If the disabled individual is to develop into a person of self-worth, it is important that he associate with people who consider him a real human being. The last thing he needs is a relative, a therapist, or a doctor who literally breathes for him. He needs people who show him respect and dignity. He does not have to be able to walk or easily express himself to earn such respect and dignity. If he is director of his own life he will reveal feelings of self-confidence and self-worth. When these feelings are absent, depression, despondency, and discouragement is likely to replace them.

Society's Reactions in Perspective

The disabled individual is one of society's prime targets when it comes to expressing negative attitudes. This fact cannot be denied. It is a normal reaction from the public. Society invariably reacts to the unusual whether it involves a person, an object, or a philosophy of life. The public does not discriminate as to whom their target is. Their reactions are spontaneous. For example, people will crane their necks to look at another person who has an odd haircut or who is wearing outlandish clothing.

When people on the street stare, it cuts right through to the disabled individual's soul. The pain it can cause is unbearable. The disabled individual's only alternative is to become conditioned to the public's stares. He has to bring himself to understand why people gape. If he can understand that people are not necessarily staring at him as a person, but are staring to satisfy their curiosity about his "different" body behavior, the impact will be less.

The intensity of people staring can become less if the disabled individual realizes that there is nothing he can do to prevent it. Everybody has a right to stare at the unusual. Therefore, people have a right to stare at the disabled individual's "different" physical behavior. Staring is a privilege of both the nondisabled and disabled individual. The disabled individual also has a right to stare at anything he chooses. This impulse is uncontrollable. Everybody stares on impulse. Try as he may, the disabled individual will never be able to control the public's stares.

Presenting a "poor me" attitude gets the disabled individual nowhere. This type of attitude causes the public to react negatively. A disabled person who expresses a "poor me" attitude makes it easier for society to cope. It is when society is asked to respect such a person that they are at a loss and are uncomfortable. They are more comfortable handling an individual who does not exhibit behavior similar to theirs. Having to make the effort to accept someone who might be classified as normal is actually more difficult.

The acceptance of the disabled population is not ensured when they overstep their boundaries. Making outlandish requests for services and items which, they hope, will make their lives easier can be an irritant to the average person. The disabled individual is not doing anything to improve his role within society. If anything, he is making his place in society more complicated.

Many of the requests made to society by disabled individuals are often interpreted as a cry for pity. The public does not react favorably when they feel bombarded by mass demonstrations and telethons. Nor do they typically like being solicited for money by a television in the privacy of their homes. They are willing to help the disabled, but want to do it in their own way, and at their own time.

Stress Can Be a Dominating Problem

Frustration, conflict, and pressure are three sources of stress. They are especially common in the disabled individual's life. How detrimental stress can become is controlled by the disability's severity. The more severe the disability, the more intense the stress. Although the individual is medically advised to avoid unnecessary stressful situations, it is not always easy for the disabled individual. A disability, in itself, can cause stress. It can cause feelings of frustration. Being unable to go where he wants to go, and do what he wants to do cause immeasurable stress for the individual.

Social frustration is a typical source of stress. It requires the individual to evaluate himself realistically. This is not an easy job for every disabled individual. It is frustrating to discover all at once that, because he is disabled, he is looked down upon by everyone with whom he comes in contact. Social requirements customarily are based on standards applicable to the nondisabled. However, when the disabled individual finds that he cannot measure up to the standards of the nondisabled, his social frustration starts to mount.

Pressure is another source of stress. Its basis can be internal or external. Internal pressures occur as a result of internal desires. External pressures arise from the expectations of others. For example, a disabled individual who is surrounded by people trying to convince him that he can walk if he would just try, is put under a great deal of pressure. His stress levels become more intense if the individual believes he can overcome his disability enough to be able to walk, drive a car, or dance.

Stress experienced by the physically disabled individual differs from the stress experienced by the nondisabled individual. One reason is that the disabled individual encounters stressful situations more frequently. Since periods of extreme stress lead to emotional maladjustment one has to ask why there is no proven relationship between a disability and stress. Research leads us to believe that there is a such relationship but, it has yet to be psychologically validated. The professionals who could validate it are hesitant about deeply investigating the source of the problem. Only when such an investigation is conducted will there be a better understanding of the disabled individual.

Are You a Second-Class Citizen?

Classifying the disabled individual as a second-class citizen is unfair. There are many in society, however, who blatantly do it. Few understand that it is not how a person physically conducts himself that warrants such a classification, but that his social and emotional behavior are the determining factors. How a person gets about, whether he can or cannot use public transportation, or whether he finds a job easily are not reliable reasons for labeling a disabled person second-class. Many able-bodied persons have difficulty finding a job, getting about by themselves, and using public transportation, yet these people are usually not classified as second class. Someone who is temperamental and arrogant, and cannot get along with people, certainly warrants being in the second-class category. Similarly, the physically disabled individual who exhibits irrational behaviors should be classified as second-class.

Society should not be blamed entirely for classifying the disabled individual. The individual, himself, must accept some of the blame. I say to those I see in my practice who bemoan the fact that someone has told them they are second-class: "If you don't want to be called a second-class citizen, then don't act like one." What I mean by this is for the individual to act his age emotionally and socially. If he acts otherwise then, regardless of having a disability, he deserves to be classified as second-class.

Nondisabled One Day, Disabled the Next

Like the chronically disabled person, the newly disabled person also faces challenges. Until the day he was diagnosed as disabled, he never envisioned that these types of challenges would confront him. Now his life is riveted with challenges that demand his attention. How he comes to handle these challenges will determine how well he adjusts to the disabled world.

When an individual first becomes aware that he will be disabled for life, he experiences feelings with which he is not familiar. Intense psychological trauma sets in. Feelings of personal worth begin to suffer. Positive concept of self is threatened. The individual goes in search of the person he knew himself to be. When he cannot discover that person it causes even more anguish and frustration. As he becomes aware of this different reality, he is apt to spend hours mourning his physical losses. Unrelenting focus on negative aspects of his disability take over. Depression, hopelessness, and frustration begin to penetrate his thought processes.

Should the adult have to get about by himself in a way that is dramatically different from his past, he must face this truth. Trying to shield him from this truth borders on cruelty. The individual must realize from the very beginning that medical facts are just that. He must face the fact that there is no pill that can guarantee his disability will be erased from his life.

The case of Tracy points out the importance of psychological adjustment as a part of total rehabilitation. Thirty-year-old Tracy, a competent wife, mother, and reliable employee, was a well adjusted young woman before contracting multiple sclerosis. The traumatic impact of the disease distorted her psychological profile. It became more difficult for her to fulfill her goals in life. She gave up on herself, stopped eating, and refused to take medication or go to therapy. Day-by-day living had no meaning.

It was not until Tracy went to counseling that she was able to work through her feelings of depression, hostility, self-grief, and daily apathy. Only then did her physical, emotional, and social outlook on life change. She dared to look at herself as physically disabled. Tracy began to envision what her future life might be like. These positive steps in adjustment made it possible for her doctors and therapists to begin her rehabilitation program.

Had Tracy been allowed to succumb to distorted psychological attitudes, all the medication and therapy in the world would not have helped her. Tracy had to want to help herself before anyone else could help her. Responsibility for Tracy's improvement was in her own hands. It was important that she be in control of her own life again. Tracy had to decide how much improvement she must make to once again enjoy a full life.

Society frequently has difficulty believing that a physically disabled person can live a life as full as anyone else. The public does not realize that if they give him a chance, he can do many of the same activities that the nondisabled person does. For instance, just because he cannot pick up a cup or glass without spilling its contents, should not mean that he cannot enjoy a drink with a friend. He can if he is willing to drink through a straw. The point here is that by making some adaptations, he can enjoy a drink with his friend.

The disabled adult should not think of himself as being nonsocial. He does not have to sit on the sidelines. He does, however, have to determine how he can interact. This takes realistic planning. He will become more socially adept and be able to do almost everything his nondisabled counterpart does, when he makes the effort to interact with his environment and those in it. The only difference is that he may do it in a different way. For instance, like his nondisabled neighbor, he may have to do weekly grocery shopping. The difference is that one neighbor can get to the grocery store by driving, and the disabled neighbor must be driven. The point of sameness here is that both individuals shop at the grocery store, but get there in different ways.

Contrary to what is usually thought, the disabled individual is not necessarily helpless. If he exerts a little initiative, he can do many of the activities done by the average person. Society is of the opinion that if a person cannot perform a skill like most people, he cannot do it at all. Nothing could be further from the truth. The disabled individual can do nearly everything the average person can do if he makes special adjustments. With this theory in mind, no longer can one look upon the disabled individual as totally dependent upon another.

An Inventory of Abilities Can Tell a Lot

How much an individual is able to do for himself reveals a lot about him. This is true concerning the physically disabled individual as well. Although he may not be able to do every activity his nondisabled counterpart does, there are activities he can perform. It is up to a counselor to discover them. Once discovered they can reveal how the individual feels about himself. Overlooking this aspect of an individuals personage, and not discussing it with him, leaves much to be learned.

Below is an inventory I have found to be helpful with clients, both disabled and nondisabled. The information provided gives a comprehensive picture of the individual's various potentials. Each question reveals a lot about the individual. This information is of paramount importance before any deep counseling is undertaken. Many times all the individual needs is reassurance and reinforcement of his abilities.

A. Personal-care abilities
   (1) Did you dress yourself today?
   (2) Did the weather outside influence the type of clothing you are wearing today?
   (3) Can you take a bath or shower by yourself?
   (4) Describe for me the routine you go through for bathing and dressing.
   (5) Do you shop for your own clothes?
       Does your mother buy your clothes?
   (6) At what times do you think you should wash your hands?
   (7) Can you brush your teeth?
       How often do you brush your teeth?
   (8) Can you wash your own hair?
       How often do you wash your hair?
B. Housekeeping skills
   (1) Do you live alone or with your family?

(2) Do you offer to keep the home neat?

(3) What would you do if the kitchen sink got stopped up or the toilet in the bathroom backed up onto the floor?

(4) What might cause such an incident?

(5) What would you do if you saw bugs on the ceiling in your bedroom?

(6) Who would you call for help?

    a. Sink was clogged.

    b. Something was broken.

    c. The heat was not working.

(7) Who does your laundry?

Could you do it yourself?

C. Public transportation, leisure time, and community resources

    (1) Have you ever traveled on a bus by yourself?

    (2) How did you learn where to go?

    (3) If you wanted to know what was going on in your community, who might you contact? Where would you look?

    (4) Have you ever done grocery shopping?

    Is there a grocery store near your home?

    (5) If you're home alone in the evening what do you do?

D. Emotional and behavior characteristics

    (1) Do you have any friends?

    If so, do you spend a lot of time with them?

    (2) Do you ever have any problems with people around you?

    How do you solve such problems?

    (3) If you like a person, how do you tell him that?

    (4) If you have a disagreement with someone in your home, how do you settle it?

    Do you argue with them, do you just do nothing about working out the disagreement?

    (5) How do you handle anger?

    Tell me some ways to lessen anger.

    (6) Do you ever feel angry?

    When you do, how do you get over it?

    (7) What is the difference between borrowing and stealing?

E. Feelings about self

    (1) What is your opinion of yourself?

    How would you hope other people would think of you?

    (2) Tell me how you feel about having a disability.

(3) Do you sometimes get discouraged and feel sorry for yourself?

(4) Do you feel people think of you as a cripple, or do you feel they think of you as a normal person who happens to be disabled?

(5) What do people say or do to you that really makes you mad?

(6) How do you wish people would treat you?

What the Law Says

It is crushing for disabled adults to realize that they have no source of financial income. This is common because they often cannot find employment, are considered unemployable, or are told by family members that they must just adjust to their circumstance. This can cause the disabled individual to feel unimportant. It does nothing to improve his concept of himself. If anything, it only justifies the thoughts of self-depreciation he already has developed.

One reason the disabled adult often finds himself in financial straits is that he is not familiar with various disability benefits. It is likely that no one has informed him of them. It is more likely that members of his family do not know, themselves, about the benefits. In an attempt to rectify this, the following is the latest information regarding disability rights provided by the Social Security Administration. Although the benefits will never turn a disabled individual into a millionaire, they can serve to lessen his feelings of poverty. It is strongly recommended that those working with disabled individuals bring these disability benefits to the individual's attention and help them to apply.

Social Security Disability Benefits: Who Should Read This Information?

You should, if you want to know more about the various kinds of disability benefits available from Social Security. This booklet will tell you who may get benefits, how to apply, and what you need to know once benefits start.

We pay disability benefits under two programs: the Social Security disability insurance program and the Supplemental Security Income (SSI) program. For most people, the medical requirements for disability payments are the same under both programs and a person's disability is determined by the same process. While eligibility for Social Security disability is based on prior work under Social Security, SSI disability payments are made on the basis of financial need. And there are other differences in the eligibility rules for the two programs. This booklet deals primarily with the Social Security disability insurance program. For information on SSI disability payments, ask at any Social Security office for the booklet, SSI (Publication No. 05–11000)

Please Note: This booklet provides a general overview of the Social Security disability insurance program. The information it contains is not intended to cover all provisions of the law. For specific information about your case, contact Social Security

Social Security's Toll-Free Number 1-800-772-1213

Internet: www.ssa.gov

Part 1 Introduction To Disability and Social Security
What We Mean by "Disability"?
Who Can Get Disability Benefits?
How Much Work You Need?

Part 2 Signing up for Disability
How Do I Apply?
How Can I Speed up My Claim?
Who Decides If I Am Disabled?
How We Determine Disability?
Rules for Blind Persons
If My Claim Is Denied

Part 3 When a Claim Is Approved
When Do My Benefits Start?
How Much Will I Get From Social Security?
How Other Payments Affect My Benefits.
Are Benefits Taxed?
Can I Get Medicare If I'm Disabled?
Is My Case Reviewed?
What Can Cause Benefits to Stop?

Part 4 Going Back To Work
Can I Receive Benefits While I Work?
For More Information
Other Booklets Available

Disability and Social Security

Disability is something most people don't like to think about. But the chances of your becoming disabled are probably greater than you realize. Studies show that a 20-year-old worker has a 3-in-10 chance of becoming disabled before reaching retirement age.

It's a fact that, while most people spend time working to succeed in their jobs and careers, few think about ensuring that they have a safety net to fall back on should the unthinkable happen. This is where Social Security comes in, we pay cash benefits to people who are unable to work for a year or more because of a disability. Benefits continue until a person is able to work again on a regular basis, and a number of work incentives are available to ease the transition back to work.

What Do We Mean by "Disability"?

It's important that you understand how Social Security defines "disability." That's because other programs have different definitions for disability. Some programs may pay for partial disability or for short-term disability. Social Security does *not*.

Disability under Social Security is based on your inability to work. You will be considered disabled if you cannot do work you did before and we decide that you cannot adjust to other work because of your medical condition(s). Your disability also must last or be expected to last a year or to result in death.

This is a strict definition of disability. The program assumes that working families have access to other resources to provide support during periods of short-term disabilities, including workers' compensation, insurance, savings, and investments.

Who Can Get Disability Benefits?

You can receive Social Security disability benefits until age 65. When you reach 65, your disability benefits automatically convert to retirement benefits, but the amount remains the same.

Certain members of your family may qualify for benefits on your record. They include:

- Your spouse who is age 62 or older, or any age if he or she is caring for a child of yours who is under age 16 or disabled and also receiving checks.

- Your disabled widow or widower age 50 or older. The disability must have started before your death or within seven years after your death. (If your widow or widower caring for your children receives Social Security checks, she or he is eligible if she or he becomes disabled before those payments end or within seven years after they end.)
- Your unmarried son or daughter, including an adopted child, or, in some cases, a stepchild or grandchild, The child must be under age 18 or under age 19 if in high school full time.
- Your unmarried son or daughter, age 18 or older, if he or she has a disability that started before age 22. These children are considered disabled if they meet the adult definition of disability. (If a disabled child under age 18 is receiving benefits as the dependent of a retired, deceased or disabled worker, someone should contact Social Security to have his or her checks continued at age 18 on the basis of disability.)

For more information about disability benefits for children, ask Social Security for the booklet, *Benefits or Children With Disabilities* (Publication No. 05–10026).

Note: The Supplemental Security Income (SSI) program also pays benefits to many disabled children under age 16.

How Much Work You Need

To qualify for Social Security disability benefits, you must have worked long enough and recently enough under Social Security. You can earn up to a maximum of four work credits per year. The amount of earnings required for a credit increases each year as general wage levels rise. Family members who qualify for benefits on your work record do not need work credits.

The number of work credits you need for disability benefits depends on your age when you become disabled. Generally you need 20 credits earned in the last 10 years ending with the year you become disabled. However, younger workers may qualify with fewer credits. The rules are as follows:

- Before age 24—You may qualify if you have six credits earned in the three-year period ending when your disability starts.

- Age 24 to 31—You may qualify if you have credit for having worked half the time between 21 and the time you become disabled. For example, if you become disabled at age 27, you would need credit for three years of work (12 credits) out of the past six years (between age 21 and age 27).
- Age 31 or older—In general, you will need to have the number of work credits shown in the chart shown below. Unless you are blind, at least 20 of the credits must have been earned in the 10 years immediately before you became disabled.

Born after 1929, Become Disabled at Age	*Credits You Need*
31 through 42	20
44	22
46	24
48	26
50	28
52	30
54	32
56	34
58	36
60	38
62 or older	40

Part 2—Signing up for Disability

You should apply at any Social Security office as soon as you become disabled. You may file by phone, mail, or by visiting the nearest office.

How Can I Speed up My Claim?

It generally takes longer to process claims for disability benefits than other types of Social Security claims—from 60 to 90 days. You can shorten the process by bringing certain documents with you when you apply and helping us to get any other medical evidence you need to show you are disabled. These include:

- the Social Security number and proof of age for each person applying for payments including your spouse and children, if they are applying for benefits;

- names, addresses, and phone numbers of doctors, hospitals, clinics, and institutions that treated you and dates of treatment;
- names of all medications you are taking;
- medical records from your doctors, therapists, hospitals, clinics, and caseworkers;
- laboratory and test results;
- a summary of where you worked and the kind of work you did;
- a copy of your W-2 Form (Wage and Tax Statement), or if you are self-employed, your federal tax return for the past year; and
- dates of prior marriages if your spouse is applying.

Do not delay filing for benefits just because you do not have all of the information you need. The Social Security office will be glad to help you.

Who Decides if I Am Disabled?

After helping you complete your application, the Social Security office will review it to see if you meet the basic requirements for disability benefits. They look at whether you have worked long enough and recently enough, your age, and, if you are applying for benefits as a family member, your relationship to the worker. The office will then send your application to the Disability Determination Services (DDS) office in your state. The DDS will decide whether you are disabled under the Social Security law.

In the DDS office will consider all the facts in your case. They will use the medical evidence from your doctors and from hospitals, clinics, or institutions where you have been treated and all the other information they have.

On the medical report forms, your doctors or other sources are asked for a medical history of your condition:

- what is wrong with you;
- when it began;
- how it limits your activities;
- what the medical tests have shown; and
- what treatment you have received.

They also are asked for information about your ability to do work-related activities, such as walking, sitting, lifting, and carrying. They are not asked to decide whether you are disabled.

The DDS may need more medical information before they can decide your case. If it is not available from your current medical sources, you may be asked to take a special examination called a consultative examination.

Your doctor or the medical facility where you have been treated is the preferred source to do this examination but it may be done by someone else. Social Security will pay for the examination and for certain travel expenses related to it.

Our rules for determining disability are different from the disability rules in other government and private programs. However, a decision made by another agency and the medical reports it obtains may be considered in determining whether you are disabled under Social Security rules.

Once we reach a decision on your claim we will send you a letter. If your claim is approved, the letter will explain why and tell you how to appeal if you don't agree.

How Do We Decide Disability?

You should be familiar with the process we use to determine if you are disabled. It's a step-by-step process involving five questions. They are:

1. **Are you working?** If you are and your earnings average more than $700 a month, you generally cannot be considered disabled. If you are not working, we go to the next step.
2. **Is your condition "severe"?** Your condition must interfere with basic work-related activities for your claim to be considered. If it does not, we will find that you are not disabled. It it does, we will go to the next step.
3. **Is your condition found in the list of disabling impairments?** We maintain a list of impairments for each of the major body systems that are so severe they automatically mean you are disabled. If your condition is not on the list, we have to decide if it is of equal severity to an impairment on the list. If it is, we will find that you are disabled. If it is not, we go to the next step.
4. **Can you do the work you did previously?** If your condition is severe, but not at the same or equal severity as an impairment on the list, then we must determine if it interferes with your ability to do the

work you did previously. If it does not, your claim will be denied. If it does, we go to the next step.

5. **Can you do any other type of work?** If you cannot do the work you did in the past, we see if you if you are able to adjust to other work. We consider your medical conditions and your age, education, past work experience, and transferable skills you may have. If you cannot adjust to other kind of work, your claim will be approved. If you can, your claim will be denied.

Rules For Blind Persons
You are considered blind under Social Security rules if your vision cannot be corrected to better than 20/200 in your better eye, or if your visual field is 20 degrees or less, even with a corrective lens.

There are a number of special rules for persons who are blind. The rules recognize the severe impact of blindness on a person's ability to work.

For example, the earnings limit for people who are blind is generally higher than the $700 limit that applies to non-blind disabled workers. This amount changes each year. For current figures and other information on special rules for persons who are blind, ask for the leaflet, *If You Are Blind . . . How We Can Help* (Publication No. 05–10052).

If My Claim Is Denied
If your claim is denied or you disagree with any part of our decision, you may appeal the decision. The Social Security office will help you complete the paperwork.

You have 60 days from the time you receive our letter to file an appeal. We assume that you receive the letter with our decision five days after the date on it, unless you can show us that you received it later. For more information about appeals, ask for the factsheet, *The Appeals Process* (Publication No. 05–10041).

Part 3—When a Claim Is Approved

When Do My Benefits Start?
If your application is approved, your first Social Security benefits will be paid the sixth full month after the date your disability began. Because Social Security benefits are paid in the month following the month for which they're due, benefits for January are paid in February and so on.

You also will receive a booklet, *What You Need To Know When You Get Disability Benefits* (Publication No. 05–10153), in case you have questions.

How Much Will I Get from Social Security?

The amount of your monthly disability benefit is based on your lifetime average earnings covered by Social Security. If you would like an estimate of your disability benefit, all you have to do is call or visit Social Security and ask for it. We'll send you a form you can use to get a personal earnings and benefit estimate statement. You also can get the form from our Internet website: www.ssa.gov.

How Do Other Payments Affect My Benefits?

Eligibility for other government benefits can affect the amount of your Social Security benefits. The following publications provide more information and are available form Social Security.

- *How Workers' Compensation And Other Disability Payments May Affect Your Benefits* (Publication No. 05–10018).
- *A Pension From Work Not Covered by Social Security* (Publication No.05–10045).
- *Government Pension Offset* (Publication No. 05–10007), a law that affects spouse's or widow(er)'s benefits.

If you have additional questions, contact your local Social Security office, or call us toll-free at 1-800-772-1213.

Other Disability Benefits

Social Security benefits may be affected if you are also eligible for workers' compensation (including black lung) or for disability benefits from certain federal, state, local government, Civil Service, or military disability programs. Total combined payments to you and your family from Social Security and any of these other programs generally cannot exceed 80 percent of your average current earnings before becoming disabled. (Note that for income tax purposes, your unreduced benefit is counted.)

Government Pension Offset

If you are a disabled widow or widower or the spouse of a disabled worker, a "government pension offset" may reduce your Social Security payment. The offset applies if you become eligible for a federal, state, or local government pension based on your own work not covered by Social Security.

The amount of your Social Security spouse's benefit may be reduced by two-thirds of the amount of your government pension. There are some exceptions when the offset would not apply. For more information, call or visit Social Security to ask for a free copy of the fact sheet, *Government Pension Offset* (Publication No. 05–10007)

Pension from Work Not Covered by Social Security

If you become disabled and entitled to a Social Security disability benefit and you also receive a monthly pension based on work not covered by Social Security, your disability payment will be smaller than normal. That's because we use a different formula to figure the Social Security benefit of people who get other public pensions. For more information, call or visit Social Security to ask for a free copy of the factsheet *A Pension from Work Not Covered by Social Security* (Publication No. 05–10045).

Are Benefits Taxed?

Some people have to pay federal income taxes on their Social Security benefits. This usually happens only if your total income is high. At the end of the year, you will receive a Social Security Benefit Statement (Form SSA-1099) showing the amount of benefits you received. Use the statement is to complete your federal income tax return if any of your benefits are subject to tax. For more information about this tax, ask the Internal Revenue Service for a copy of Publication 915. Also, you may choose to have federal taxes withheld from your benefits.

Can I Get Medicare If I'm Disabled?

We will automatically enroll you in Medicare after you get disability benefits for two years.

Medicare has two parts—hospital insurance and medical insurance. Hospital insurance helps pay hospital bills and some follow-up care. The taxes you paid while you were working financed this coverage, so it's premium free. The other part of Medicare, medical insurance, helps pay doctors' bills and other services. You will pay a monthly premium for this coverage if you want it. Most people have both parts of Medicare.

Help For Low-Income Medicare Beneficiaries

If you get Medicare and have low income and few resources, your state may pay your Medicare premiums and, in some cases, other out-of-pocket Medicare expenses such as deductibles and coinsurance. Only your state can decide if you qualify. To find out if you do, contact your state or local welfare office or Medicaid agency. For more general information about the program, contact Social Security and ask for the leaflet *Medicare Savings For Qualified Beneficiaries* (HCFA Publication No. 02184).

Is My Case Reviewed?

In general your benefits will continue as long as you are disabled. However, we will be review your case periodically to see if you are still disabled. The frequency of the reviews depends on the expectation of recovery.

- If medical improvement is "expected," your case will normally be reviewed within six to 18 months.
- If medical improvement is "possible," your case will normally be reviewed no sooner than three years.
- If medical improvement is "not expected," your case may be reviewed no sooner than seven years.

What Can Cause Benefits to Stop?

There are two things that can cause us to decide that you are no longer disabled and to stop your benefits.

Your benefits will stop if you work at a level we consider "substantial." Usually, average earnings of $700 or more a month are considered substantial.

Your disability benefits would also stop if we decide that your medical condition has improved to the point that you are no longer disabled.

You must promptly report any improvement in your condition, your return to work, and certain other events as long as you are receiving benefits. These responsibilities are explained in the booklet you will receive when benefits start.

Part 4—Going Back to Work

Can I Receive Benefits while I Work?

If you're like most people, you would rather work than try to live on disability benefits. There are a number of special rules that provide cash benefits and Medicare while you attempt to work. We call these rules work incentives. You should be familiar with these disability work incentives so you can use them to your advantage.

For more information about Social security work incentives, ask for a copy of the booklet, *Working While Disabled . . . How We Can Help* (Publication No. 05–10095).

CHAPTER 5

Challenges the Professional Faces

Make no mistake about it, like other working people, rehabilitation professionals face challenges. They deal with as many mind-boggling challenges as the families of disabled individuals, and the individuals themselves. Sometimes it is overlooked that doctors, therapists, and other professional health-care workers are human beings like everybody else. They go home at the end of the day mentally exhausted from trying to do their best for a disabled individual. They sometimes go home with heavy hearts because they had to tell a parent that his child will be physically and mentally disabled for life. The professional telling such sad news may also be a parent. This, of course, does not make the job any easier. He cannot help but remind himself how fortunate he is that his boy or girl is not disabled.

One of the most difficult challenges rehabilitation doctors and counselors deal with is the individual who becomes obsessed with his disability. Trying to converse with him is difficult. He persists in negative thinking. In fact, such thinking takes over his mind. He becomes convinced that there is no hope for him. It takes a special skill to remove this barrier between the disabled individual and the professional. The professional should engage the individual in conversation about himself. If the conversation does not center around his disability, the beginnings of a mutual "friendship" can develop.

A man who has just acquired a disability and must begin walking with crutches yearns to get rid of the crutches and be able to dance with his wife again. The young girl who has just acquired a spinal injury wonders who will drive her Corvette now. Will her family sell it? Or, will they give it to her younger brother? A six-year-old child in a wheelchair yearns to get up and run with the neighborhood children.

Each of these individuals burns with a desire to do what he or she will likely never be able to do. They may express their rebellion loudly or silently live with it. Whichever, it is strong and unrelenting. Feelings of worthlessness can cancel out any possibility of developing positive attitudes. Feelings of hopelessness raise their heads and can last a lifetime. Their attitude of hopelessness blocks out any light at the end of their tunnel.

It is important that professionals extend maximum understanding to the disabled individual. He needs an understanding ear to listen to how he feels. When he feels that the professionals understand him, he is more likely to cooperate in therapy programs. Only then will he agree to take prescribed medications. And, only then, will he show psychological stability. Although this understanding will not erase a physical disability, it can provide a better chance for the individual to function at his best.

There are few medical conditions that cause the psychological trauma experienced by an individual when told he may be disabled for life. Becoming aware of how different his physical behavior may appear to others can emotionally shake him. Concept of self becomes distorted, and the disability's characteristics engulf every waking hour of his day. It becomes easy to convince himself that he is not useful or important to anyone, including himself. His psychological outlook on his life and society as a whole takes on an abnormal tinge.

The longer the individual harbors a negative concept, the more difficult it will be to improve himself physically, mentally, psychologically, or socially. He will lack self-confidence, self-initiative, and the ability to direct his own life. Looking down at his disabled body, he sees no hope. He sees no chance of improving physically or psychologically. For him to exist day by day is a chore. Rather than hoping his condition will improve, he wonders how much worse it can become.

What Is Psychological Rehabilitation?

The discipline of medicine and physical, occupational, and speech therapies make up the standard rehabilitation program. Whereas these areas of treatment each are of paramount importance, psychological rehabilitation is just as important and should be added to the list of disciplines.

The psychological problems that a disability causes can be more debilitating than many physical problems. Psychological problems last longer and are more traumatic. Sitting in a wheelchair all one's life can be more upsetting than the disability itself. The wish to move about like other people is psychologically debilitating.

To cancel out some of the disability's impact, the individual should be told why he is in a wheelchair. Explanatory information can give him a realistic reason for having to be in a wheelchair. It provides him with an opportunity to make a better adjustment to the disability. It is when this information is withheld that the physically disabled adult is likely to enter a stage of psychological turmoil.

Professionals involved in directing the rehabilitation of the disabled child or adult must recognize the role that they play in maintaining the disabled individual's will to survive. Only then can the individual think of his disabled body as a body that might serve him well. Rehabilitation personnel must also develop an accurate concept of a disabled body. It is essential that they view the body as one crying out for their understanding and compassion. It is important to keep in mind that although the body in question may not do what is demanded of it, it is a body housing a human soul. A disability is no reason to consider the individual less than a human being. Like everyone else, he reacts emotionally to life's circumstances. He gets hurt, he can feel happy or sad, and he responds to the same worries that trouble everybody else.

The physically disabled individual cannot reach successful solutions to problems as fast as the average person. If a disabled person is to be successfully rehabilitated the two disciplines plus the three therapies previously suggested must be utilized. The most important discipline should be psychological followed by medical. The three therapies should be considered in this order: physical, occupational, and then speech. Although some individuals may only need treatment in one or two of these areas, every individual needs treatment in the psychological area.

Regardless of whether the disability is severe or not, the individual experiences psychological trauma. This would be true of anyone. Psychological comfort levels drop when a person realizes that his life may be changed forever. It is important to recognize that psychological comfort levels can plummet without any previous notice. The individual can wake up one morning and feel as if his whole life has fallen apart.

An important ingredient for good adjustment is that the individual feel psychologically comfortable in his body. When these levels are at low ebb, the individual feels down on himself and uncomfortable in his body.

The desire to improve himself comes to a halt. Nothing can improve his attitude overnight. Shoving a pill down the individual's throat, therapeutically moving his arms and legs back and forth, or performing any other kind of therapy on his body will not have positive results. More is accomplished when the individual can approach his exercises with a positive attitude. The individual must be psychologically ready before he will be able to cooperate in a treatment program. This makes it imperative that psychological and medical disciplines, as well as physical, occupational and speech therapies, be considered a vital part of every rehabilitation program.

The Rehabilitation Team

The therapeutic goal of the rehabilitation team is to strengthen the disabled individual's growth and development in many areas. In some instances ordinary rehabilitation techniques have to be used and not altered in any way. In the majority of cases, the stigma of being different can be minimized if the psychologist, doctor and therapist treating the individual work together as a team. A team that works well together can provide a surrogate family atmosphere, which in turn, provides a sense of security.

Importance of Preserving Dignity and Modesty

A cardinal rule in all rehabilitation is to preserve the dignity and modesty of the disabled individual. Failure to do this is an act of blatant disrespect. Frequently, the disabled individual's dignity and modesty is taken for granted. He, as a human being, is often considered and treated as insignificant by rehabilitation personnel. They place so much intent on meeting his rehabilitation needs that they forget they are treating a human being.

Many times personnel overlook the fact that for an individual to lie half naked on a gurney, or for him to be quizzed about his intimate body parts, is a source of embarrassment. Just because he cannot pull a sheet up over himself does not mean that his pride and dignity should not be preserved. However, when he does verbally try to preserve his dignity and modesty, the nurse or therapist, or even the doctor, telling him not to worry about it can be also embarrassing to him. Being spoken to in such a pitying manner shows a lack of respect for the disabled individual. He senses that the caregivers interest in him is only on whether he can move his legs or arms. He feels that not wanting his body exposed to the whole wide world is of no significance.

Another area where the disabled individual is not shown respect by professionals is in the conversational area. Professionals tend to be excessively emotional. They do not dignify the disabled by addressing him as Mr., Miss, or Mrs. Instead, they resort to infantile language. Perhaps this is because they are uncomfortable in his presence, do not know what to say to him and, yet, want him to feel comfortable in their presence. Thus, they say to the individual, "Come on, sweetie. You can do it. Do it for me, dear." However, for a twenty or thirty year old adult to have to listen to such remarks tells him the low status of his dignity in the speaker's mind. Addressing him by his name, or by Mr. or Miss, is far more acceptable to the disabled individual.

Compatible Rapport Essential to Progress

A positive rapport between the disabled individual and his rehabilitation therapist is essential. If the relationship is totally controlled by the therapist or doctor, and no recognition is given to the disabled individual's feelings, he will rebel during the treatment session. He will refuse all treatment. His concept of the rehabilitation process becomes distorted. These are normal reactions. No one enjoys being controlled by another person. Most people want to function on their own. They want to have some say about what is done to them and how it is done. This is true whether it is in a medical environment or in a vocational environment.

The disabled individual and his therapist must develop mutual respect and understanding if any significant progress is to be made. If they do not, therapy is a lost cause. The effects of a compatible relationship between the two can be outstanding. This is particularly true of the newly disabled individual. To be consulted by specialists interested in his welfare, at probably the lowest time in his life, helps to develop the individual's first positive feelings. It can help cancel out feelings of negativism. If his treatment is administered in an austere manner it can have opposite results. The individual may develop the feeling that someone has taken over his life, his body, and is daring to predict his future. Under these circumstances, the individual may feel compelled to justify himself by being hostile toward the treatment therapist.

Parents Should Seek Help

Some parents rear their disabled child with little or no difficulty. Others do not. There are many factors that influence the ability to rear such a child with minimal problems. Age of the parents, self-esteem, number of children, socioeconomic status, and the severity of the disability are just a few.

In cases where the disability proves to be a point of contention, family counseling can be helpful. Parents should not, however, consider their need for help as a black mark against them. It should be looked upon as a source of assistance that can noticeably lessen the stress and pressures on them. It is not unusual for parents to need help in dealing with feelings of isolation, depression, and conflict. These feelings can interfere with their ability to care for the child. Cognitive therapy can provide family members the opportunity to examine their feelings, understand them, and eventually find solutions for them. Many parents need supportive therapy and this should come as no surprise to professionals. Parents need to vent their concerns related to their disabled child.

Unfortunately, the anguish of parents does not diminish as the child gets older. Every day they look at their disabled child they feel a twinge of sorrow in their heart. It is not unusual for them to have periodic recurrences of sadness, grief, and depression known as the "chronic sorrow syndrome." If these feelings of sadness and grief of many years past, interfere with the parents ability to function, psychological counseling can be helpful.

Family therapy can serve two purposes. It can help both the parents and family members make a satisfactory adjustment. Parents are making a wise move when they submit to professional help in handling their feelings of hate, grief, denial, and even their wish to kill the child. Refusing help can do long-term psychological damage to the parent and to the child. More feelings of peace and comfort are gained when disturbing feelings are laid out on the table and discussed.

Parents of a disabled child will continually come into contact with a host of professionals. This is par for the course. It will be necessary for appointments to be made with medical specialists, psychologists, special-education teachers, and therapists. These professionals become important to the family and the child. In line with their expertise, each professional will explain to parents the results of any evaluation he has made of their child. Parents are helped immeasurably when professionals offer them specific forms of help. Various treatment options should be offered. Teaching parents intervention and advocacy strategies are just a few ways of helping.

It is important for parents to become a part of the child's treatment program. Whether or not a child reaches his maximum potential should not be determined by therapists alone. Professionals should encourage parents' interest in their child's treatment program. This is contrary to what took place in years past when professionals told the family what to do, whom to go to, and what to say. In those days, the family was not consulted regarding their child's treatment program.

Empowering parents to be able to help their child is essential. This is the approach I have used for years in my practice with all types of parents. Parents are consoled when their feelings are accepted by an understanding counselor. After all, a parent of any child can only be helped to solve the problems of rearing the child if he wants to solve them. The other advantage is that empowering parents to help themselves results in a beneficial partnership between the professional and themselves.

Professionals can give parents strength when they empower them to take part in their child's treatment planning. Granted, when this is the case, parents are more apt to challenge and question the information given them. It is a good sign when they do. Every parent needs to feel that he can vent his feelings without being criticized. When he does, he becomes more relaxed.

The opposite is true when a parent feels that advice is being crammed down his or her throat. This is when parents are more likely to balk and be difficult for professionals to handle. Parents are more at ease when they feel professionals recognize that to have a disabled child is not an easy experience.

Behaviors That Can Challenge Professionals

All children have behavior problems. However, the disabled child's problems are more involved. For example, the palsied child may have impairments that prevent him from having a good walking balance or good sitting balance. Another child may have impaired or retarded speech. These problems can cause the child to be aggressive, hostile, and difficult to handle.

Aggressive Behavior
The type of aggression exhibited by a child is determined by the problems he has to solve as he grows up. Signs of aggression appear in all

children because of periodic needs to satisfy specific goals. The older aggressive child teases or strikes his playmates. His aggressive behavior differs from that of the non-disabled child. He has a driving compulsion to establish his worth as a person in the eyes of others. This grows stronger as he grows older.

The problems that a ten year old disabled child is solving are frequently so overwhelming that he approaches them with a negative attitude. If he is pushed to do something that is too difficult for him, he reacts with negative aggression. Should a child have difficulty speaking, he may express his aggression in a subtle manner. Bed wetting or spitting out food are common aggressive behavior examples. The intelligent disabled child who cannot physically act out his aggression may resort to these techniques.

Daydreaming

Disabled children who are unable to compete with the nondisabled frequently daydream. Since they cannot do what they see others doing, they withdraw from reality into their own private world. They conjure up images of the self they wish to be. They see that self running up and down the street, playing and doing all the things other children do.

Daydreaming can have a dramatic affect on a child's learning ability. In fact, it can retard it. A child who daydreams exerts superficial efforts in therapy and in his school work. The daydreamer concentrates poorly and retains little of what he is taught. Regardless of the severity and type of disability, a child must be encouraged to become self-entertaining and independent. He must be provided with food for thought to give him healthy thinking habits. A busy mind has little time to escape into daydreaming.

Withdrawal

A child who has not adjusted to the fact that he is different from other children withdraws from the world. If he has been assured that he can do everything other children do, that he is no different from other children, his parents have not given him protection against the day when he realizes the full impact of his disability. When this day comes, the jolt can make him withdraw completely or become bitter and hostile. He may suddenly decide there is nothing good about him. He may try to make himself completely objectionable. Chances are he will be ostracized from group activities. Few children welcome another child who can adversely affect their relationships with other children.

It is not only the child with a severe disability who withdraws. A child with a mild disability suffers also. Parents can easily fall into the trap of discounting their child's mild impairment, pressing him to perform as well as a normal child.

Temper Tantrums

All youngsters at one time or another exhibit temper tantrums. There are many causes for tantrums. With the average child it usually is a way of getting attention. This can be just as true in the case of the disabled child.

In many instances, however, the basis for the tantrum can be frustration or a desire to accomplish something but being physically incapable of doing it. In other instances the cause may be unsuccessfully trying to make himself understood. In this case the more he is misunderstood the stronger the tantrum becomes. This can be true of the youngest of children as well as the disabled teenager or young adult. Temper tantrums increase as a disabled child's level of frustration rises. If he is unable to speak clearly, he may pound on a table, kick over a chair, scream, or yell.

If temper tantrums are a common occurrence, and the disabled child or teenager will not lend himself to talking out his frustrations, the best thing to do is to let him get it out of his system. Put him in a room by himself and give him a pillow to hit and throw around. This technique will get across to him that you recognize his predicament and that at the same time you are giving him a chance to beat it out of his system. This works well with the child who cannot easily express himself in any manner.

Using a Disability as an Excuse

Excuses! There are few individuals who at one time or another have not tried to hide a fault behind an excuse.

The disabled child or teenager, be he mildly or severely involved usually can conjure up a good excuse to hide behind. The range is wide: a child throws his dinner plate on the floor at mealtime, a teenager or young adult does not try to do his best in school or on a job, or takes no pride in his grooming. With the child it might be easy to say, "Stop using your handicap and get down to doing this." But with the older individual it may be necessary to be more direct by pointing out his faults and letting him know that his disability should not be an excuse for avoiding a skill he is able to do.

What the Law Says

Many professionals are not familiar with the laws applicable to the disabled population. The truth of the matter is that many of these laws can be of assistance to the families of the disabled as well as to the disabled individual himself. Following is one of the more recent and important laws that is applicable to many different areas of the disabled's life.

P.L. 101–336, The Americans with Disabilities Act of 1990

The Americans with Disabilities Act (ADA) was signed into law by President Bush on July 26, 1990. The central purpose of this Act is to extend to individuals with disabilities civil rights protections similar to those provided to individuals on the basis of race, sex, national origin, and religion. Based on the concepts of the Rehabilitation Act of 1973, the ADA guarantees equal opportunity for individuals with disabilities in employment, public accommodation, transportation, state and local government services, and telecommunications. The ADA is the most significant federal law ensuring the full civil rights of all individuals with disabilities.

Title II of the ADA prohibits discrimination on the basis of disability by state and local government entities. Office of Civil Rights (OCR) is responsible for enforcing Title II with respect to all programs, services, and regulatory activities relating to the operation of public elementary and secondary education systems and institutions, public institutions of higher education and vocational education (other than schools of medicine, dentistry, nursing, and other health-related schools), and public libraries.

Title II regulations are found at 28 Code of Federal Regulations (CFR); Part 35. For additional information and answers to questions regarding the ADA, contact the ADA Regional Disability and Business Technical Assistance Center. See "Organizations" at the end of this publication for contact information. For specific information on the requirements of Title II that are applicable to public school districts, public institutions of higher education and vocational education (other than schools of medicine, dentistry, nursing, and other health-related schools) and public libraries, contact the Office of Civil Rights regional office that serves your state.

CHAPTER 6

Getting Educated Is Possible

The physically disabled child presents a multitude of complex problems to teachers and school administrators. The average child rarely presents these problems. The child who has poor standing balance and appears as if he will fall when he tries to walk creates concern to those around him. Immediately, everyone's sympathies are aroused. This is particularly true of teachers.

Teachers have not been told how much better it is for the disabled child if they are unemotional in their handling of him. During their training teachers have not been advised of the psychological impact a disability can have on a child's total development. Like everyone else, teachers have a tendency to pity the child. This does not help a disabled child.

A teacher must be able to interpret correctly the psychological reactions a disability causes. When she does, she is providing the disabled child an opportunity to develop self-assurance and independence. She recognizes the child as one with the same emotional reactions that make up the personality of an average child. *It is also important that she recognize that the child is a disabled child.* The teacher of the special child must become aware of how the psychological impact from a disability can influence the ability to learn. Poor physical coordination, poor speech ability, or an unbalanced walking gait, all have specific psychological effects on the child.

When teachers recognize the vital effect these factors have on the ability to learn, they do not allow those factors to control a child's comprehension ability. The teacher should understand that even though a child cannot write out his schoolwork he should be helped to develop the "will-to-do." When this phrase becomes embedded in his mind, he will make the effort to master all skills. If, on the other hand, the teacher allows the disability to become a stumbling block it will have a detrimental affect on the child's ability to learn.

The disabled child can learn to act like other human beings if he is encouraged to interact socially with his environment. Social interaction helps the child develop a healthy concept of self. Even so, the disabled child may not fit easily into play groups. He has to be taught how. *His inability is not because he cannot physically fit in but because he cannot socially fit in.*

Importance of Early Education

The younger the physically disabled child is exposed to a school classroom the better it is for him. The child who begins his education at three years of age, has an advantage over the child who enters the classroom at six or seven years of age. Putting a young child in a classroom environment has many advantages. One is that his intellectual abilities are tapped. He is exposed to activities similar to those introduced to the nondisabled three- or four-year-old. He learns how to think for himself, and how to handle himself in the environment.

There is also an advantage for the parent. Placing the child in a classroom environment exposes him to many factors that can be helpful in motivation of his desire to learn. For instance, monthly parent meetings provide an opportunity to learn of the latest techniques for handling such a child. These meetings also introduce the newest equipment for use with the disabled child.

The disabled child who has not had a preschool experience, will be more apprehensive about starting school. He is more apt to feel threatened in a group of children when he does not know them. This new experience may confuse him. He may have difficulty finding his place in the strange environment. This child is more likely to be a behavior problem in the classroom. His learning abilities may be significantly immature when compared to the child who has experienced preschool.

Importance of a Sound Relationship between Teacher and Child

Teachers of the nondisabled child are to be accountable for what they teach. This is a cardinal rule of education. It applies also to the education of the physically disabled child. No longer are they allowed to sit in the classroom and weave potholders. Today this type of education is considered antiquated. Instead the teacher must be accountable for what she teaches the disabled child, whether he is mentally retarded or not. Due to this mandated accountability, it has been discovered that a child with severe physical problems can often exhibit unusual learning ability.

The same theory applies to a child's social ability. The younger a child is required to act in a socially acceptable manner, the more likely he will do so. A twelve-year-old disabled child is old enough to be integrated into a classroom with nondisabled children the same age. Every child, regardless of his disability, should be encouraged to interact with others the same age.

Parents' Influence on the Learning Process

Some disabled children are apathetic when they first enter school. Others demand attention. One child may fear being in the classroom environment, another tries to control the environment. There are some children who adjust well and there are other children who approach every activity in the classroom with a negative attitude. How any child, disabled or not, initiates himself into the learning experience has a direct bearing on how he has been handled in the home.

The case of ten-year-old Bobby describes this fact very well. The statement made by his mother sets the stage. "Bobby never causes me any trouble at home. I can sit him anywhere, give him a toy, and he is as happy as a lark." The truth of the matter was that Bobby's mother never made him do anything for himself. All he had to do was ask and everybody jumped to bring him things. It was imperative that the teacher understand this. Bobby's mother catered to his every need, therefore, adversely affecting his total development.

The mother was told that unless this situation was remedied, Bobby would remain psychologically and emotionally immature. At the age of twenty-one he would be a child in an adult body. Even though he was able to get about by himself in a wheelchair, Bobby had never developed any skill abilities. If he wanted a picture colored, it was colored for him. He was given a drink of water whether he asked for it or not. His toileting was kept on a stringent schedule. The food he was fed at mealtime was the choice of his mother. Because he lacked an opportunity to make decisions for himself, it became obvious that Bobby would be difficult to handle in the classroom.

The teacher began to counteract Bobby's immaturity by insisting that he do as much as possible for himself in the classroom. For example, if he wanted anything he was to roll himself over and get it. When it was time to go home, although Bobby insisted that his teacher put his hat and coat on, the teacher gave him his hat and told him to put it on his head. Since it was obvious to everyone that Bobby could not button his coat, the teacher did that for him. Her only requirement of Bobby was that he do as much as he could for himself.

During class time, Bobby was never put at a table and given baby work to do. If he sat at a table, he was given a purposeful activity to do. His teacher made a point of tapping Bobby's intellectual abilities every minute of the school day. In six weeks' time there was a noticeable improvement in Bobby's psychological and emotional maturity. He began to experience what it was like to be director of his own thinking. It was up to him to ask for a drink of water when he wanted one or to tell someone when he had to go to the bathroom. He also began to show interest in reading and math. Soon he would tell anyone offering to do things for him to leave him alone and let him try to do it. He made his teacher's day when she was coloring a picture for him and he looked at her and said, "Don't. I can do it myself." Bobby's confidence in himself grew and he began to feel self-assured.

It is not the physically disabled child's inability to walk and talk like other children that prevents him from accomplishing skills. For example, parents often are quick to assume that because their child cannot walk or talk, he also is unable to learn. Yet, it is while learning to do skills for themselves that all children get the urge to learn. Sometimes the child's disability interferes with his ability to learn. Another reason is that he does not have the opportunity to benefit from other children's experiences. He becomes a victim of people's insatiable desire to help him.

After High School Graduation, What?

After graduating from high school, a lot of young people go to college. After college they look for a job. Their objectives are to be independent of their families, have their own money to spend, and prove successful in finding a job of their own choice.

The physically disabled person makes every effort to follow the same pattern. Even though his objectives are the same as the nondisabled young person, they are more difficult to fulfill. For instance, looking for a job can be a disheartening experience for the disabled young person. His application may be turned down many times. If he goes for an interview, the minute they see that he is disabled his chance of being employed is unlikely. This may be the first time he is forced to realize that because of his disability he may have trouble getting a job in a field of his choice.

If the individual cannot write with a pencil, cannot easily operate a computer keyboard, or cannot get about on his own, his career choices are limited. He certainly is not eligible to be a teacher. Although he may possess the intellectual skills, he does not possess the physical skills to pursue such a career. If he has understandable speech, he might be good at doing research for a publisher of classroom workbooks. If he possesses some ability to operate a computer keyboard, there might be a place for him in a library. He might be able to label cards or type labels for different book categories on the shelves.

This can be equally as true for the individual whose disability may only be unintelligible speech. He certainly is not the best candidate to be a trial lawyer. It may be necessary for him to reevaluate his professional priorities. He may have to choose another area in the legal profession that does not require a lot of speaking ability. Perhaps he could prepare data for a court session. Working in legal research might be another possibility. The main objective is to find an area of interest in his chosen field that lends itself to the necessary adaptations for his limited abilities. The answer certainly is not to give up. It does require careful planning when entering college.

A disabled individual frequently is not provided with adequate vocational counseling prior to going to college. Instead, he is encouraged to pursue any career of his choice. That he may not be able to function fully in that career is overlooked. It is the individual who must realize that his disability can be the problem preventing him from getting the job he wants. Being forced to become aware of one's flawed capabilities is a devastating experience for anyone.

Is College for Every Disabled Person?

Not every young person is college material. Some go to technical school, others go right out after high school and find a job. Others enter college. If the person does not have the intellectual ability to do college work he should not be encouraged to attend. Forcing him to do so puts him in a compromising position, particularly if he has a disability. If attending college will require him to exert an unusual amount of energy to keep up with classmates, perhaps he should not go. Like his nondisabled counterpart, the physically disabled person should have a good reason for wanting to attend college. It should not be promoted only so the family can be free of his care. Colleges are not baby-sitting agencies although some families use them as such. If the disabled student is to attend college it is essential that he do some realistic planning.

Getting a college degree just to get a degree has no valuable purpose for anyone. A college degree that merely hangs on a bedroom wall has no meaning. If the purpose of the degree is finding employment, it then has a productive value. This is what John's parents told him as he prepared to go off to college.

In his case, vocational counseling spared him much disappointment. Although John lies prone on a gurney, he was determined to become a certified public accountant. His first love was working with figures. Thus, upon entering college he naturally enrolled in the accounting department. The department's misguided professors made no effort to stop him. The consensus of opinion was that if John could do the work intellectually, they had no right to put barriers in his way. They overlooked the fact that he would never be able to sit up at a desk or perform other on-the-job activities.

During the first week of college, one of the professors who would have John in his class spent some time counseling him. He pointed out to John that he would never be able to sit up and write figures in an account book. Being unable to go to an office every day was another problem brought to his attention.

At first John resented the counseling. It ruined all the ideas that he had for his future. It made him face up to facts about himself that he had made great efforts to ignore. He could not envision himself as anything other than a certified public accountant.

Eventually John had to face the truth. He could no longer kid himself into thinking that he could become an accountant. It was suggested to John that he leave the accounting department and seek a degree in business journalism. This area of study had more adaptable possibilities. In time, this new interest proved worthwhile.

Once his works were published, John became a successful writer for leading business journals. His assignments appeared throughout the world. Although John was unable to type out his articles or enter them on a computer, he made enough money from their royalties to hire someone to transcribe for him. No, he did not make enough to pay a mortgage on a home, but he did make enough to support himself, pay for help to conduct his business, and pay a small stipend to his parents with whom he shared his home. The important thing in John's case was that his four years of college were not wasted. Upon graduation he was able to enter into the profession he had prepared himself for.

Making the Right Choice

For those disabled individuals who wish to attend college, there are a growing number of such institutions to accommodate them. For example, Boston University has a special program for disabled students. If a student must use a wheelchair the Americans with Disabilities Act (ADA) of 1990, PL 101—336, mandates wheelchair accessibility of most classrooms in colleges. This was not true in years past. A disabled student entered college hoping he could adapt to the program with little difficulty. If he could not handle the program, he was asked to leave the campus.

There are a number of catalogs that list the colleges accepting physically disabled students. Among them is *"The K&W Guide to Colleges For Students With Learning Disabilities or Attention Deficit Disorders"* published by Princeton Review Publishing, L.L.C., 2315 Broadway, New York, New York 10024. It is suggested that disabled students consult this catalog. For those students who may need financial assistance to go to college, or for any other reason, it is recommended that they consult: *"Financial Aid for the Disabled and Their Families 1998-2000"* by Gail Ann Schlachter and R. David Weber. It is published by Reference Service Press, El Dorado Hills, California.

The prospective disabled student should seek a counselor's help to determine what college to attend and what program to enter. To go off to college without such an evaluation is poor planning. The college programs in which a disabled individual can be successful, depend upon the severity of his disability and how the disability may limit his performance. If he cannot take notes with a pencil, or operate a cassette player, arrangements should be made before entering college to supply such assistance. If he cannot go to the library himself, arrangements have to be made for someone to take him.

Twenty-one-year-old Abby is a case to consider. Although she did superior academic work in college, her severe physical limitations proved to be a problem when she started to look for a job. Being unable to feed herself and toilet herself were serious drawbacks. That Abby was unable to work on a computer keyboard without lying on the floor to balance her arms was another problem. Nevertheless, she was determined to become an elementary teacher.

The college she attended overlooked her physical limitations and had allowed her to sign up for courses in the education department. No one told Abby how her disability could interfere with her dream of becoming a teacher. She developed an unshakable faith in her abilities and was left to discover this heartbreaking reality herself. Having been praised by professors for four years as being a student with honor grades, she found it difficult to discriminate between her academic abilities and her physical abilities. After graduation she was intent on selling her teaching techniques. She saw no reason why she should even mention her physical drawbacks. Thinking realistically about herself was not on her agenda at this time.

Abby left no stone unturned. She sent out applications to various school districts. Since they did not require her to state that she was disabled, she only gave her exceptional academic record as proof of ability. This was a normal procedure, one that any other college graduate would follow. However, when Abby had to let them know that she was disabled, they withdrew their interest quickly.

Abby fell into a deep depression and seriously began to question her own abilities. She wondered if the college had just given her good grades because she was disabled. She heard that had happened to some disabled students. She could not bring herself to face the fact that her job rejections were a result of her disability. When efforts were made to help Abby find a more suitable placement in the teaching profession, she rejected them. In her mind, she had trained to become an elementary teacher and that was what she intended to become. Obviously Abby was never able to fulfill this goal. It took her many months to realize the truth.

Had an attempt been made in the beginning to help Abby prepare for a more realistic career, she would have been spared much heartache, depression, and disappointment. According to law, trying to force an individual to change her mind is infringing on her equal rights. This may be true; however, it does not always benefit the individual. The career a disabled individual pursues will determine the quality of his future life. If that pattern is to be productive then he should prepare for a career in which he has a good chance of succeeding. The disabled college student who can say to himself and others, "I would like to be a doctor, or a lawyer, or a teacher, but I am too disabled to fill those positions," is a student who is knowledgeable about his disability, views it realistically, and knows well what it will or will not allow him to accomplish. He has learned to be content with his basic abilities and does not try to be someone he will never be.

Taking First Steps to College

Before the physically disabled individual considers going to college, he has to address the same concerns as his nondisabled counterparts. If he is to be successful in college this is necessary. Going to college is a major step toward preparing for life. In the case of the physically disabled student, preparation should be realistic, down to earth, and tailored to his specific needs.

The potential disabled college student should give serious thought to the following suggestions. Answering these questions truthfully can make his adjustment on campus much easier.

(1) Could I handle myself well in a large college?
(2) If I chose a college where there are men and women, would I be too distracting?
(3) How would I feel about being away from home? Can I trust myself to stay away from home for a lengthy period of time?
(4) Am I ready to leave home and chase escalated academic demands or would it be better if I remained home and was a day student at a community college?

(5) Do I have the high school credits and grades required to enter a four-year college?

(6) How much should I tell the college administration about my disability? Should I mention it at all? Should I outline my physical limitations?

(7) Am I capable of taking care of myself health wise, c, would I need someone to check me over every so often?

(8) Due to my physical inability to write or to operate a computer easily, will I need someone to transcribe assignments for me?

(9) Will there be someone on campus assigned to me to act as a service provider who can mediate for me if the faculty does not seem to understand my point of view?

(10) Does the college I am thinking of attending offer the types of experiences as well as the academics that will help me choose a vocation?

Be Honest about Your Disability Traits

Few people are knowledgeable about disabilities and their various characteristics. This is particularly true of college administrators. They must be made aware of the specific disability characteristics of a potential disabled student. Below are seven points the disabled individual should candidly reveal to college administrators before he enters the college.

(1) Describe your disability in detail.

(2) What type of treatment do you take for it?

(3) Describe how you have learned to meet different demands in light of your disability.

(4) State disability related needs regarding test taking and other academic accommodations needed.

(5) What skills have you developed as a result of your disability?

(6) Describe the relationship, if any, between your disability and your academic records.

(7) Describe how you personally feel about your disability and its impact on your life.

Facts College Students Should Understand

Mainstreaming and inclusion in the secondary schools, coupled with efforts to eliminate architectural barriers at the post secondary level have allowed physically disabled individuals to pursue a higher education. Increasing numbers of these individuals see higher education as a means for realizing their career goals and gaining independence. However, before this can become a reality, the understanding and support of faculty and staff is essential to each physically disabled student's success.

The Career Access Center in the Department of Education at Columbia Basin College in Washington state has graciously shared their information on this subject with the author. It is from The Disability Resource Manual that the following information was gathered.

Introduction

According to the 1992 U.S. census report, there were 49 million Americans with disabilities. This means nearly one in five Americans has a disabling condition affecting a major life function.

Legal Implications for Higher Education
Federal Legislation

Section 504 of the Rehabilitation Act of 1973 and the ADA prohibits discrimination against individuals with disabilities.

According to these laws, no otherwise qualified individual with a disability will, solely by reason of his or her disability, be excluded from the participation in, be denied the benefits of, or be subjected to discrimination under any program or activity of a public entity.

"Qualified" with respect to postsecondary educational services means "a person who meets the academic and technical standards requisite to admission or participation in the education program or activity with or without reasonable modifications to rules, policies, or practices and with the removal of architectural or communication barriers or the provision of auxiliary aids and services."

"Person with a disability" means any person who: (1) has a physical or mental impairment that substantially limits one or more of major life activities (including walking, seeing, hearing, speaking, breathing, learning, and working); (2) has a record of such an impairment, or (3) is regarded as having such an impairment.

General Suggestions

Every person has limitations. Likewise, even students with disabilities have the potential to overcome limitations if given a fair opportunity. Therefore, educators should not overestimate those limitations and accommodate the student beyond what is reasonable. Students with disabilities should be viewed as individuals rather than as "they," "those," "them," or "the handicapped."

Do not overprotect students with disabilities. While this may be very difficult for many sensitive, caring persons to accept, making choices, even poor choices, is an important part of total development and maturity. Faculty and staff members need to provide plentiful opportunities for success and a supportive environment for the student facing a challenge. The objective is not to eliminate the experience of failure but to capitalize on its potential for learning.

Expect the student with a disability to meet the same standards of academic performance as all students. Students are in college because of their abilities, not their disabilities.

Make a general announcement at the beginning of class to all students and include a statement on the class syllabus inviting students to discuss academic needs. Instructors can avoid difficulty later on by stating their willingness to discuss individually any student's special needs as early in the class as possible. Doing so might encourage some students whose disabilities are not readily discernable to vocalize their needs. An example of such a statement may read: "If you are a student with a disability and you need accommodations, please make an appointment with me to discuss these needs."

Do not apply blanket accommodations. Needs vary much among individuals, even those with the same disability. Therefore, all accommodations are not automatically applicable to all students with a particular disabling condition. A disability can vary in terms of the degree of limitation, the length of time the person has been disabled, and the stability of the condition.

Do not feel students with disabilities are getting unfair advantages. Students with disabilities do not get by with less work. Often, they must work harder than the non-disabled student.

Do not be afraid of saying or doing the wrong thing. By avoiding communication or contact with a person with disabilities, fears and misconceptions cannot be curbed. Discomfort can and will ease if persons with disabilities and those without disabilities interact with each other more often in school, work, and social settings.

Recognize that a student with a disability may afford you a unique opportunity. What is not always readily appreciated is the unique input of a person whose life experiences are different from the norm. The very fact that any student has chosen to come to college is a statement of a desire to learn and to contribute.

Remember that a disability does not automatically prevent a student from participating in certain activities or classes. For example, a student with a visual disability may benefit from an art class with certain modifications and adaptations. A student without the use of his or her hands can learn the process and results of a chemistry experiment. Moreover, advances in computers and assistive technology are opening up more possibilities at an extremely rapid rate.

Just ask! By asking students if they need assistance, you are giving them the option to accept or deny help. Respect, however, each individual's desire for confidentiality. Some students do not wish to disclose their disability or do not want accommodations. This is their right. It is the instructor's responsibility to inform students that accommodations are available.

Talk directly to the student with a disability. Comments such as "does he or she want to . . ." should be avoided. Even when a deaf student is using an interpreter, look at the student and direct all questions and comments to the student.

Teaching Students with Disabilities

- At the beginning of each term, let all students know how they can request accommodations.
- Provide students with a detailed course syllabus and make it available before class starts, if possible.
- Announce reading assignments well in advance for students who are using recorded materials.
- If possible, allow students with disabilities to demonstrate mastery of course materials using alternative methods.
- Start each lecture with an outline of material to be covered that period. At the end of class, briefly summarize key points.
- Present new or technical vocabulary on the blackboard or use a student handout. Use terms in context to convey greater meaning.
- Provide study questions for exams that demonstrate the format as well as the content of the test. Explain what constitutes a good answer.
- Reinforce lectures or discussions by putting major topics or outlines of the material on the board.
- Give assignments both in writing and orally to avoid confusion.
- Encourage the student to ask questions during or after class to insure that materials are understood.

- Frequently verbalize what is being written on the board.
- Offer as many sensory modalities as possible (e.g., visual, auditory, tactile, kinesthetic).

Traumatic Brain Injury

The effects from traumatic brain injury (TBI) vary greatly. Most head injuries can cause impairment in memory; conceptualization, cognition, perception, communication, spatial reasoning, and executive functions (e.g., goal setting, planning) as well as motor, sensory, and physical abilities. TBI can affect psychosocial behavior, including denial, emotional lability, impulsivity and disinhibition, apathy, frustration, lack of insight, verbosity, intolerance, confabulation, lack of initiative and follow-through, inefficient and slow thinking, poor judgement and reasoning, and social imperception.

Many of these psychological difficulties may be a result of a brain injury and are part of a student's disability. Students with such disabilities need to know, however, they are expected to follow the school's code of conduct and will not be permitted to disrupt a classroom or other campus situation to the detriment of other students.

Teaching Students with Traumatic Brain Injury

Many of the teaching techniques that aid students with learning disabilities also benefit those with TBI. Specific suggestions include:

- Avoid overstimulation.
- Be consistent.
- Remain calm—observing others' calmness can help to reduce confusion.
- Give step-by-step directions—this enables all students to have less confusion and feel more successful.
- Talk to a student with TBI at his or her age level —his or her intellect is still intact.
- Incorporate frequent repetition of information to be learned and emphasize memory cues, such as a calendar and daily logs.
- Allow additional response time—this gives the TBI student the opportunity to think through the material.
- Give praise, when appropriate —everyone needs encouragement.

Mobility Impairments

The term *mobility impairment* refers to a broad range of disabilities that includes orthopedic, neuromuscular, cardiovascular, and pulmonary disorders. The mobility impairment may be congenital or a result of injury, muscular dystrophy, cerebral palsy, multiple sclerosis, heart disease, or pulmonary disease. Some are hidden (nonvisible) disabilities that may include physical limitations. While the causes may vary, students with mobility-impairments may have to contend with such difficulties as:

- Decreased physical stamina and endurance.
- Decreased eye-hand coordination.
- Impaired access to specific rooms or buildings.
- Decreased ability to physically write or take notes.
- Impaired verbal communication.

These barriers to learning should be considered by the instructor and reasonable accommodations discussed with the student to assist with his or her success.

Interaction with Students with Mobility Impairments

- Accept the fact that a disability exists. Not acknowledging the disability equates to not acknowledging the student.
- First ask if you can help, when it appears that a student with a mobility impairment needs assistance. Most students will ask for assistance if they need it, and may resent it otherwise. Be prepared for, and accept, a "no thank you" graciously.
- Do not assume that a student who uses a wheelchair only some of the time mean the student is "faking" a disability. Students are generally not "confined" to wheelchairs. It may be a means to conserve energy or move about more quickly. Some students transfer to automobiles and to furniture, and can walk with the aid of canes, braces, walkers, or crutches.
- Do not pat people in wheelchairs on their heads. While intended as a gesture of affection, this can be humiliating and patronizing.
- Conversation at different eye levels is often difficult for anyone, especially for those in wheelchairs. If a conversation continues for more than a few minutes and if it is possible to do so, sit down, kneel, or squat and share eye level.
- Speak directly to the mobility impaired student as you would another student.
- Do not hesitate to ask a student to repeat or rephrase a statement if the student's speech is difficult to understand.

• Do not avoid words like *walking* or *running* in general conversation. Students who use wheelchairs use these same words.

Teaching Students with Mobility Impairments

Access to campus buildings and facilities is a major concern for mobility impaired students. Student must learn routes to and from classes and across campus that do not present barriers. A barrier can be a heavy door, a curb, a stair, a narrow walkway, a blocked ramp, or a steep slope.

The following are general considerations:

Class changes/field trips. In some cases, a student who uses a wheelchair may need to make arrangements with the instructor for special transportation.

Special Accommodations. Students should be encouraged to talk with their instructors (during the first week) to inform them of any arrangements or needs they may have to succeed in class.

Lateness and Absence. Because there is usually only 10 minutes between class periods, students with mobility impairments occasionally may be late to class. They may experience several obstacles en route, such as negotiating crowded paths and corridors, opening doors that aren't electric, or waiting for an elevator. Students and instructors may want to plan for these occasions, so important class material is not missed.

Laboratory Assignments. Students and instructors are encouraged to work together to develop methods to enable a student who has difficulty with "hands-on" work to develop accommodations.

Tests. Students should discuss any alternative test taking methods with the instructor. Alternative methods can include assigned writers if the student is unable to write. Students requesting assistance or extended time should not be asked to take the test in the hallway or other inappropriate places; a room should be provided for them. Instructors can give oral tests, or students can tape or type the answers for the test.

Note Taking. Each mobility impaired student has his or her own way of taking notes. Some will do it themselves, some will use notetakers, and others will tape record the lectures. Accordingly, you may ask a student in your class to share his or her notes with the mobility impaired student. If a notetaker is used, carbonless notetaking paper is available to make note sharing easier.

Speech Impairments

Speech impairments range from difficulty with articulation or voice strength to a complete inability to speak. Impairments can include stuttering (such as repetition, blocks, or prolongations occasionally accompanied by distorted movement and facial expressions), difficulty in expressing an appropriate word or term (minimal aphasia), chronic hoarseness (dysphonia), and esophageal speech (resulting from a laryngectomy).

Teaching Students with Speech Impairments

The extent to which a student with a speech impairment needs accommodations varies according to the individual, as is the case in any disability. Listed below are general guidelines to use for some situations.

- Impaired speech may be slower than unimpaired speech. Students with speech impairments need to have an equal chance to voice their reactions or questions even if it means allotting extra time. Some students may need extra encouragement to participate in class.
- DO NOT be hesitant to ask for repetition of words or phrases; students with speech impairments would much rather repeat a message than have the listener pretend to understand what they are saying. After listening to what was said, summarizing the message is often a helpful way of checking with the student as to whether the message was clear.
- DO NOT interrupt or try to complete the student's train of thought. An instructor trying to anticipate the question being asked can embarrass the student if the instructor's completion of the sentence was not the original question or point being made.
- After conversing with speech-impaired students, the ability to understand their speech will improve over time.
- Oral presentations may be of concern to the student and the instructor. Some students prefer to have another person voice their presentations; others prefer to do it for themselves. Instructors should openly discuss these concerns with the student.

Cerebral Palsy

Cerebral palsy (CP) is not a disease, but a condition involving nerve and motor dysfunction caused by damage to the brain. The term cerebral refers to the region of the brain that has been damaged and palsy refers to shaking or uncontrolled movement. Although, usually a result of prematurity or oxygen deficiency during birth, CP also can be caused by injury, drugs, or child abuse. Cerebral Palsy is neither progressive nor communicable.

Cerebral Palsy is characterized by an inability to control motor function. Depending on which part of the brain has been damaged and the degree of involvement in the central nervous system, one or more of the following may occur: spasms; involuntary movement; disturbance in gait or mobility; seizures; abnormal sensation and perception; impairment of sight, hearing, or speech; and in extreme cases, mental retardation.

Cerebral Palsy involves damage to motor centers only. To the uninformed, however, the unnatural movements and facial expressions are often incorrectly assumed to be signs of mental or emotional disturbance, or drunkenness. In addition to major limb impairments, individuals with CP may have hand tremors, making fine movements difficult. They may have problems in speaking, chewing, swallowing, maintaining visual focus, or following a moving target.

Teaching Students with Cerebral Palsy

Every student with Cerebral Palsy presents a unique capacity and potential for coping. A lot depends on the student, what programs are available at the college, and the student's personal support system.

Accommodations will vary for each student, depending on the severity of CP and the functional areas affected. Assistance may include using a notetaker, audio-recording lectures, alternative testing measures, and being given extended time on tests. Many of the accommodations mentioned under "mobility impairments" may also be helpful.

If Support Services Are Needed

The physically disabled college student will undoubtedly need extra support services. How much and what kind should be determined before enrolling in college. Every college does not offer the services. If the need is to be prevalent, the student should arrange for it right in the beginning of his freshman year. For example, if he cannot write with a pencil or has difficulty using a computer keyboard he should look into what the college has to offer as a substitute for him.

Due to his various physical limitations, he may not be able to keep up with the rest of the class when it comes to taking a test. He may have to ask for an extension of time when taking an examination or preparing a class project. Or, another student may need a reader for taking his exams, someone who can read the exam to him. Transcribers may also be needed to write the answers to the exam if the student has to take it in this manner.

In the first year of college, some disabled students find it wise to take a modified schedule. It might be easier to take four courses rather than six in the beginning until he gets well acclimated to college life. While taking fewer courses may extend his time in college, the fact that taking a modified program of courses will benefit that student should not be overlooked. It is better for him to do well with fewer courses than to fail miserably because he overloaded himself. This is another decision that should be made before enrolling. The final decision should then be registered with the college administrators.

Preregistration may be another wise move for the physically disabled student. If he cannot get about easily he may benefit by registering for his courses before the whole student body descends on campus. Advisors are more apt to be available early in the registration period to help the disabled student. Should he be easily confused by multiple impressions and get frustrated easily, he certainly would if he registered as one of 800 or 1,000 students.

What the Law Says

Following is the often-cited law assuring disabled children a public education. Too often the wording of this law, and how it works, is not known by parents. It is important for parents to know that there is a law that assures their disabled child the same educational rights as the nondisabled child.

P.L. 94–142, Education for All Handicapped Children Act of 1975

This law was passed in 1975 and went into effect in October of 1977 when the regulations were finalized. This law strengthened earlier acts of a similar name, including P.L. 91–230 and P.L. 93–380. Ballard, Ramirez, and Zantal-Weiner (1987) and DeStefano and Snauwaert (1989) summarize the major purposes of P.L. 94–142 as:

To guarantee that a "free appropriate education," including special education and related service programming, is available to all children and youth with disabilities who require it. To ensure that the rights of children and youth with disabilities and their parents or guardians are protected (e.g., fairness, appropriateness, and due process in decision-making about providing special education and related services to children and youth with disabilities). To assess and ensure the effectiveness of special education at all levels of government. To financially assist the efforts of state and local governments in providing full educational opportunities to all children and youth with disabilities through the use of federal funds.

In 1983, through the Education of the Handicapped Act Amendments of 1983 (P.L. 98–199), Congress amended, or changed, the law to expand incentives for preschool special education programs, early intervention, and transition programs. All programs under EHA became the responsibility of the Office of Special Education Programs (OSEP), which by this time had replaced the Bureau of Education for the Handicapped (BEH).

In 1986, EHA was again amended through P.L. 99–457, the Education of the Handicapped Act Amendments of 1986. One of the important outcomes of these amendments was that the age of eligibility for special education and related services for all children with disabilities was lowered to three, a change to be implemented by school year 1991–92. The law also established the Handicapped Infants and Toddlers Program (Part H). As specified by law, this program is directed to the needs of children, from birth to their third birthday, who need early intervention services. In addition, under this program the infant or toddler's family may receive services that are needed to help them assist in the development of their child. State definitions of eligibility under this program vary.

In 1990, Congress passed the Education of the Handicapped Act Amendments of 1990 (P.L. 101–476). The new amendments resulted in some significant changes. For example, the name of the law, the Education of the Handicapped Act (EHA), was changed to the Individuals with Disabilities Education Act (IDEA). Many of the discretionary programs authorized under the law were expanded. Some new discretionary programs, including special programs on transition, a new program to improve services for children and youth with serious emotional disturbance, and a research and information dissemination program on attention deficit disorder, were created. In addition, the law added transition services and assistive technology services as new definitions of special education services that must be included in a child's or youth's IEP. Also, rehabilitation counseling and social work services were included as related services under the law. Finally, the services and rights under this law were expanded to more fully include children with autism and traumatic brain injury.

The Education of the Handicapped Act, P.L. 94–142, and its amendments, P.L. 98–199, P.L. 99–457, and now the Individuals with Disabilities Education Act, P.L. 101–476 and P.L. 102–119, represent the most important pieces of educational legislation in the history of educating children and youth with disabilities. As has been said, parents and professionals should make every effort to familiarize themselves with these laws. The regulations that cover the Individuals with Disabilities Education Act are also to be found in the Code of Federal Regulations. They are called C.F.R.: Title 34; Education; Parts 300 to 399.

CHAPTER 7

Life Can Be Made Easier

Most people brush their teeth, comb their hair, take a shower, put on their makeup, and shave with no difficulty. These personal-care activities are often difficult for the disabled individual to do. Many have to have these tasks done for them. In many cases, if the disabled individual is to do them himself, adaptations must be made.

Independently caring for oneself encourages the development of self-worth. This is as true for the disabled individual as it is for the nondisabled individual. Every person likes to feel that he can take care of himself. Few people enjoy having someone else wash their face, brush their teeth, or comb their hair. Sometimes the embarrassment of having this done by another person cannot be put into words.

Customarily, the public judges others by what they see. The adage "you can't judge a book by its cover" is so true when it comes to how people appear in the eyes of others. If they are slovenly groomed and are careless with their personal hygiene, others will reject them. This does not only apply to the nondisabled, but also to the disabled individual.

Flashy styles of grooming may not be suitable for disabled adults. Whereas the disabled individual hopes it will improve his chances of being accepted by nondisabled peers, it often does not. In fact, if he chooses to wear flashy styles, rather than cause him to be positively recognized, it can make his disability conspicuous. The disabled woman who dresses like a "Plain-Jane" or a gentleman whose style falls into the "straitlaced" category, will create the opposite appearance. If the disabled adult chooses a style of grooming, not too flashy or too conservative, he is exercising good taste.

Equally as important is the choice of hairstyle. Some of the current styles do little to improve anyone's appearance. Nevertheless, for a disabled girl with limited arm motion, long hair may be impractical. One reason is that it requires someone to comb it every day. If on the other hand, she wears her hair short, she may be able to take care of it herself.

Jean found this to be true. She had long hair. Although it was becoming to her, her mother or sister had to comb it every time she wanted to go out. This, however, was only one problem her long hair presented. Jean also needed assistance to wash it. Once she was convinced that she would look just as well with short hair and be more independent by taking care of it, she never let her hair grow long again.

The same problem exists in the case of young men. Wearing a crew cut is much easier to take care of than a ponytail style. The latter can become straggly and messy. The same is true of wearing a beard. It requires daily upkeep. Ignoring this can result in an unkempt appearance.

Taking Good Care of Oneself

For the disabled individual to have a good perception of himself is essential. However, many disabled individuals do not. Frequently, the individual is so bogged down with the problems stemming from his disability that developing a good vision of himself is doubtful. The disabled individual who does not have a good image of himself acts as if he does not fit in anywhere. Undoubtedly this is the way he pictures himself in his mind. He thinks negatively about himself and physically appears negative. He is careless with his personal hygiene. He does not care how he appears to others or how they think of him. His tendency is to appear just as he mentally thinks of himself.

One reason for this is that no one has told him how to do it. No one has taken an interest in helping him shop for attractive clothes, purchase necessary personal toiletries, or made sure his shoes were shined. Those around the individual usually are so engrossed in his disability that they fail to recognize that he does have other needs. These needs are, many times, just the same as those of his nondisabled counterpart. When the disabled individual is inspired to improve his perception of himself he will do so. He must do so if he wants to be a member of society otherwise he will be classified as a second-class citizen.

The quality of care that the disabled individual gives to himself is important. This quality, however, is based upon the individual's concept of himself. If the concept is good, the quality of care will be good. If the concept of self is poor, the quality of care will leave much to be desired. The individual with a good concept of himself will bathe everyday, shave everyday, and wash his hair at least once a week. The female individual will ask to have her nails manicured, make sure her makeup is neatly applied, and take pride in her grooming.

Self-Care Abilities That Make Life Easier

How well a physically disabled child cares for himself depends upon the type and severity of his disability. Some children are better at taking care of their own hygiene than others. One child may walk well enough to get himself a drink of water, while another child, who cannot walk, has to have the water brought to him.

Toilet training is another area demanding special attention. The disability's type and severity determine how easily this job can be accomplished. One child may be able to toilet himself and only need help with the zipper and buttons. Another child may need considerably more help. In either case, the child should be trained to do as much as he can for himself. Preserving his dignity and pride should also be considered. Toileting the disabled child in any room of the house does not preserve his dignity or pride. Early toilet training should begin in the bathroom, not on a potty chair in the kitchen or the living room.

The same training procedures should be utilized when teaching a child how to get a drink of water. At the ages of four, five, and six years, it should not be necessary for someone to have to ask the disabled child periodically if he wants a drink. He should be able to indicate in some manner when he wants a drink of water. Training the child to accept such responsibility makes him conscious of his personal needs. He becomes aware of himself as a person. Having to be totally dependent upon others deprives him of the ability to act like other children.

Soap and Water Never Hurt Anyone

Personal cleanliness should be a priority in everyone's life. It certainly should be in the life of the physically disabled person. It not only makes him more acceptable to other people, but it contributes to his health. Some people shower every three days, others need to take a daily shower. Whichever schedule is followed, both can be applied to men and women, disabled or not.

Daily hygiene practices are also important. If the individual must exert a lot of physical energy, body odors may occur at the least provocation. Difficulty walking or any other kind of excessive physical movement can result in body perspiration, which in turn can cause body odor. Thus, a daily shower or bath is in order. If he cannot do this himself, someone in the home should be assigned to help him.

It is often said of a disabled individual, "He is an awful nice person and I do enjoy talking to him but I cannot stand being near him because of his body odor." The importance of good personal hygiene cannot be overstated. To insure acceptable relationships with others, the disabled individual should make every effort to be clean and odorless.

Like any other individual, the disabled individual's teeth require a yearly check up as well as daily care. Even though the individual may not be able to walk or speak intelligibly, he still needs to have regular check ups. Teeth needing attention can cause bad breath, poor health conditions, as well as detract from one's appearance. Proper dental care can also be a factor in improving speech impairments.

Grooming Can Improve Psychological Outlook

People are judged by their appearance, which includes grooming and personal hygiene. This is profoundly true in the case of the physically disabled individual. If he appears neat and well-groomed, society is more apt to accept him. If he wears scuffed shoes, unpressed clothes, and gives a general appearance of being unclean, society is more apt to reject him.

To be well-groomed does not mean that one has to be expensively groomed. All good looking clothes are not purchased at Saks Fifth Avenue. Equally attractive clothing can be purchased at J. C. Penney's, K-Mart, or Sears and Roebuck. If clothes are always cleaned and ironed they will appear presentable, and thus there should be little to criticize.

Wearing attractive clothing often reveals how one feels about himself. It can indicate if he is happy or sad. The disabled individual reacts in the same manner when he looks down at himself and can tell himself that he looks neat. This is a great step toward developing a healthy ego. The teenager tells himself that even though he may not walk or talk as well as his peers, he is dressed as well as they are.

Too Much Makeup Can Detract

Average and disabled women have something in common. They both wear makeup. The desire to improve one's appearance is normal. The problem arises when too much makeup is applied.

If applied with moderation, makeup can be an asset to the physically disabled woman's appearance. Heavily applied makeup is unattractive on any woman and particularly so on a disabled woman. A desire to highlight personal attractiveness is normal. The important thing is that it be skillfully applied. If it is not, it can make a disability more noticeable and attracts more attention. Sensibly applied makeup does just the opposite.

Suggested Adaptations of Personal "Tools"

Adapting the ways and means for the disabled person to care for himself independently takes a lot of ingenuity on the part of family or the individual, himself. For instance, one person may find a big soap mitt easier to wash his face and body with than a washcloth and a bar of soap that slips out of his hands. Another individual may find it difficult to grip a toothbrush. It may be easier to use an electric one. If the brush is correctly introduced, and the tooth cleaner stabilized in front of the individual, this allows him to rub his teeth back and forth over the bristles without worrying about holding onto the brush. Still another disabled person may find it easier to use tooth powder by dipping it into a cup or shaking it onto the brush. Many find doing this much easier than grabbing and squeezing a tube of toothpaste. Likewise, a solid deodorant may make less of a mess in poorly coordinated hands than a liquid deodorant.

Activities of Daily Living

Male and Female Tools

- Elastic waistbands on trousers with belts sewed over the elastic can look as if a belt is being worn.

- Elastic shoelaces that do not have to be untied can make slipping shoes on and off an easy job.
- Neckties knotted in advance and placed on rubber can easily be slipped over the head.
- Rubber placed in shirt cuffs will make it unnecessary to button tiny buttons.
- Hidden zippers under the buttons on a shirt front can make a boy self-sufficient.
- Velcro that has to be pressed on to close or pulled apart to open can be put on the front of an overcoat (with the buttons left in their ordinary place).
- Undershorts with elastic waistbands are helpful.
  Short-sleeved T-shirts and turtleneck shirts are easy to put on.
  Cardigan sweaters or slip-over V-neck sweaters are easy to put on.
- Velcro on clothing (replace small buttons).

Recreational Tools

- Paperback vs. hardback books (lighter weight, easier to handle).
- A pocket-sized cassette (good for taping notes or keeping reminders).

Household Tools

- *Railings in the bedroom.*

  There is nothing more frustrating for the disabled individual than being unable to move conveniently in her own room. Installing railings in one part of the room, or entirely around the room, can eliminate this difficulty. For the teenaged girl, installing railings is especially important. She cannot be expected to want to look feminine unless her personal things are readily available. If she cannot get about by herself, she may not exert herself to do things that will add to her femininity. With the railings she will be able to dress herself more easily and select her own clothes—first steps toward becoming mistress of herself.
- *Low shelves or drawers.*

  Bureau drawers that stick are not for the disabled individual who has trouble pulling a drawer out and keeping her standing balance at the same time. She may have enough trouble getting herself into position to pull even the easiest sliding drawer out. Another difficulty for the girl who sits in a wheelchair is drawers that are too high.

To remedy this, the legs of the dresser can be sawed off, lowering it to wheelchair height, or low shelves can be installed. The latter may be the simplest solution.

- *Straws.*

   If the disabled individual cannot pick up a glass of liquid without spilling it and must drink everything through a straw, he must make sure that he has straws with him wherever he goes. There are even silver-plated straws that are appropriate for evening events. Paper and plastic straws wilt or melt in hot liquid; glass straws do not and are easier to keep sterile and clean.
- *Light on and off by push button.*
- *Solidifying soup with crackers so it will not spill.*

Legal Tools

- *Identification card.* Same as license everyone has to apply for, but this card "license" is not to be used as a driver's license.
- *Use of signature stamp.* In place of writing signature with pen.

Bathroom Tools

- *Advantages of body wash.* Easier than trying to grab a bar of soap.
- *Using a mitten for soaping.* In place of a bar of soap and washcloth.
- *A rubber bath mat is a good idea.* To prevent a nasty fall.
- *Electric toothbrush.* May be easier than using standard toothbrush.
- *Toothpaste and shaving cream in a pump rather than a tube.*
   Easier to control amount.
- *Toothpowder.* Sprinkling may be easier than controlling squeezing of tube.
- *A hair-dryer on a stand can be helpful.*

Bedroom Tools

- *Hangers on pulleys.*

   No girl should throw her clothes around the room. If she is disabled she should want to keep them as neat as any other girl. For her to do so, by herself, it may be necessary that adaptations are made for this purpose, particularly in the bedroom. If the individual is immobile, if she has an artificial arm, or if she has poor standing balance, it may be difficult for her to reach up to get a hanger, place her dress on it, and hang it up again. There are several ways this difficulty can be minimized.

Installing a clothes bar that can be placed low enough so that it can be easily reached from a wheelchair is helpful. If the individual is lucky enough to have a walk-in closet, clothes hooks can be put around it just high enough so she can easily put her hangers on them. If she is in a wheelchair, she might back the chair into the closet to hang her clothes up. If she does not walk about much by herself, railings in her bedroom can be placed so they end up at the closet or in the closet itself. This can make it possible for her to hold on with one hand and hang up garments with the other.

• *Secure bedside lamps.*

Light makes a room, and the disabled girl may want the prettiest lamps on her bedside table. Her parents may be hesitant about getting them because they know that one involuntary jerk of her hand will send them crashing to the floor.

This problem can be eliminated if the lamp she selects is screwed securely to her night table. If she has trouble reaching under the shade to turn the switch on and off, the socket can be replaced by one that operates with a pull chain. Then, like any other thirteen- or fourteen-year-old, she can sneak a few more pages in her book and quickly put out the light when she hears her mother coming down the hall.

The independence obtained by such simple devices can be surprising. A teenager will no longer have to call someone to put out her light when she is ready to go to sleep. Or, if she cannot sleep, she can turn on her light and read. No one governs what she does; in one more way, she has the chance to make decisions for herself.

• *Full-length mirror.*

A full-length mirror is ideal for developing confidence in the disabled girl. She can look at herself every day before she goes to school to make sure she is neatly dressed. She should be encouraged to look at herself in the mirror to make sure she will give a neat appearance. As she gets older, she may want to sit and comb her hair in front of a mirror. This will help her develop the habit of not going out of her bedroom without looking into the mirror to check her appearance.

• *Making a dresser drawer do double duty.*

When assembling a makeup drawer there are many things to consider. It can be easier to use the top drawer of a low mirrored dresser. Even more helpful is having the bed close enough to the dresser that it can be used as a bench for seating. A lazy susan on top of the dresser can be helpful for larger bottles. They are easy to reach and the spin of the lazy susan allows access to all bottles. The use of velcro on the bottom of bottles can be helpful when reaching out with poorly coordinated hands to grab a bottle of perfume. It stabilizes the bottle on the lazy susan. Also, a good-sized, tilting, lighted makeup mirror can be helpful. It can be moved closer to the individual without having to adjust her proximity to the mirror that is attached to the dresser.

A top drawer can serve well as a "makeup table." All one's smaller bottles can be kept there. When poor coordination in the hands is a problem, perfume should not be purchased in pourable form to avoid spilling. A spray is easier to handle. Pourable lotions can be transferred into smaller squeeze bottles to limit the amount distributed. Combs, brushes, makeup and other grooming supplies fit well into this top drawer. Also a towel or washcloth can be kept to apply cleansers and lotions to the face or keep fingers clean. Deodorant can be more helpful if it is in roll-on form rather than a spray.

- *Plastic clothes hangers.* Easier to grip.
- *Sticky table top.* Can help keep items from sliding off.

Items Available from the 2001 Sammons Preston Catalog (Aids to Daily Living)

Flexible Sock and Stocking Aid:
The two long (28½") loop handles are perfect for those with limited hand function or back problems, wheelchair users, or those recovering from hip or knee surgery. Flexible plastic core makes it easy to slip sock onto trough. Lined with nylon to reduce friction. Outside is covered with terry cloth to prevent sock from slipping. Latex free.

Stainless-Steel Shoehorn/Sock Aids:
Durable stainless-steel shoehorns feature a plastic hand grip with a curved hook for pulling up socks and garments. Latex free.

Tylastic Shoelaces:
Heavy-duty elastic shoelaces for those who require or prefer better support. No special lacing or tying required. Contains latex. Two pairs per package.

Pant Clip:
Great for pediatrics through adults, the pant clip has many uses. Ideal for stroke and hip clients or those with limited mobility. This simple but effective 3″ clip attaches to pants and an upper garment while seated, then holds pants up as you stand erect. Cord adjust for height by simply tying a knot. Assorted colors: blue, teal, yellow.

Button Hooks:
These button hooks meet most buttoning needs. Ideal for those who lack fine motor coordination or have use of only one hand. Button hooks are easy to use; simply slip wire hook through button hole, grab button with wire and pull button back through hole. Several styles available. Latex-free.

Raised Toilet Seat with Safety/Hand Rails:
For those who need assistance in rising/sitting. Seat can be raised $2^{1}/_{2}$″ to $5^{1}/_{2}$″ in 1″ increments. Designed to fit regular bowls. Has a standard, unpadded seat with a circular polyethylene splash guard. Padded armrests are $7^{1}/_{2}$″ high, 18″ apart and made of 7/8″ anodized aluminum tubing. Weighs 6 lbs. Holds up to 250 lbs.

Grab Bar:
Sturdy bar can be mounted at a variety of angles for the convenience of the user. White powder-coated surface and rust resistant with a protective end cap. Requires a wall clearance of $1^{1}/_{2}$″ and gripping surface of $1^{1}/_{4}$″. ANSI/ADA recommended. Made in USA. White. Latex-free.

Bi-Level Tub Grab Bar:
Vertically oriented bar gives maximum unobstructed space for entry and exit. Tool-free installation for temporary or permanent use. Padded clamp surfaces protect tub finish and keep bar securely in place. Bi-level handgrip offers flexibility of grasp and increased safety. White. Latex free.

EZ-Bathe:
Allows clients to enjoy a bath or shower without leaving the bed. Client rolls into the vinyl tub, which is then inflated using the wet-and-dry vacuum. Tub inflates to 80″ L x 32″ W x 10″ H to accommodate individuals up to 6′2″. Fits all beds. The hand-held shower head connects to any tap up to 25′ away. Drain hose (leading to bathtub, sink or toilet) can be

turned off for a long soak or on for constant draining, allowing a constant shower. The drain hose and vac (both included) empty the tub thoroughly. (Garden hose may be used to extend tubing, if necessary.)

Curved Bath Brush:
Handle is curved 180 degrees so persons with minimal range of motion can reach their neck, shoulders, and back.

Wash Mitts:
Blue terry-cloth wash mitts with Velcro wrist closure for those with limited grasp. Plastic D-ring allows thumb to unlock the Velcro. Pocket model has a pocket with a Velcro closure to hold soap. Machine washable. Latex free.

Sponge Wash Mitt:
A sponge wash mitt with large opening that is ideal for persons with minimal hand function. Big D-ring and a Velcro closure can be fastened without grasp. Latex free.

Tabletop Mirror:
Flexible 8″ stainless steel gooseneck on stable, clear acrylic round base permits positioning at any angle.

Stand Mirror:
An easy-pivot 5″ x 4″ oval mirror that can be moved without lifting or grasping. Magnifies on one side (four diopters of magnification). Wire frame base can stand or hang. Latex free.

Telescoping Self-Examination Mirror:
Handy two-sided mirror, has regular and 2x magnification, and handle that extends from 6″–18″. Perfect for diabetics' daily foot care exam, and skin inspection in hard-to-see places. Indispensable for paraplegics and others with limited sensation. Handle collapses and mirror folds to fit into protective storage pouch. Soft-grip handle for easy non-slip grip. Shatter resistant.

Hands-Free Hair Dryer Pro Stand 2000:
Stand holds dryer steady for one-handed styling and drying, or leaves two hands free to manipulate styling instruments. Hair dryer (not included) nestles securely in foam padded clamp atop a flexible neck that can be

adjusted to any angle from its tabletop base. Ideal for hemiplegics, arthritics, and others with limited upper extremity range of motion, strength, and coordination will welcome this simple but essential piece of equipment. Increases independence in hair care for child, caregiver or self.

Long-Handled Brushes and Combs:
Great for people with limited arm or hand movement. Anti-slip handles are ergonomically designed to fit against user's entire palm. Contoured brush and comb are attractive and functional. Made of polypropylene.

Universal Electric Razor Holder:
Fits popular brand name electric razors (Sunbeam, Norelco Dual Head, and Remington Triple Head). Two Velcro straps secure the razor to a vinyl-covered, foam-padded steel handle that can be bent to fit the user's hand. (Razor not included.) Latex free.

Toothpaste Dispenser:
Attractive countertop dispenser makes it easy for individuals with limited finger/hand function or visual impairments to put correct amount of toothpaste on brush. Just align toothbrush with guide under nozzle and press long lever down with hand or arm. Toothpaste pump remains securely in place on dispenser until pump is empty. Recommended use with Aquafresh 4.3 or 4.6 oz. pump toothpaste. White plastic. Toothbrush not included.

Tube Squeezer:
Easy squeezing and less waste with the turn of a key. Assists in dispensing toothpaste, hand cream, or the contents of any tube up to 2″ wide. Slide base of tube into groove and turn the key to squeeze out the contents. Unwind key to remove the tube. Ideal for those with decreased motor skills. Plastic shell is $2\frac{1}{4}''$ round and $1\frac{3}{4}''$ high.

Dycem Nonslip Plastic
Dycem nonslip plastic helps solve many stabilization and grasping problems. Made from a specially developed polymeric compound with a uniquely high coefficient of friction. Dycem nonslip plastic is also: Nontoxic, latex free, colorfast, odorless, washes easily with soap and water, can be affixed permanently with Super glue or a neoprene 2-way contact adhesive. There are many innovative ways to use Dycem nonslip plastic.

Lightweight Utensils:
Stainless-steel utensils with $4\frac{1}{4}''$ long black nylon handle weigh only 1.1 oz. ideal for those with minimal hand strength. Dishwasher safe up to 180 degrees F. Latex free.

Weighted Plastic Base Holder:
Easy-to-grasp plastic cone-shaped base angles the utensil away from the palm to make eating easier. This holder is weighted with 8 oz. of additional weight for stability. Utensil not included. Latex free.

Heavy-Duty Utensil Holder:
Made of durable, $1''$-wide nylon webbing, this utensil holder stands up to repeated use and washings. Pocket holds assorted utensils. Velcro closure with handy D-ring makes it easy to slip on and off and adjust to MCP width $3\frac{1}{2}''$–$4\frac{1}{4}''$. Machine washable. Utensil not included. Latex free.

Universal Cuff:
Leather ADL cuff with elastic strap. Holds various utensils as well as the right-angle pocket. Sizes based on MCP width. Utensil not included.

Plate with Inside Edge:
The special inside edge keeps food from sliding off the plate to make self-feeding easier for children or adults. Plate is $9''$ in diameter with a $1''$ rim and a $\frac{1}{2}''$ edge. Colored plate ideal for identifying individuals with dietary restrictions. Dishwasher safe up to 180 degrees F and microwave safe. Latex free.

Hi-Lo Dish:
Users can push food onto cutlery against the $1\frac{3}{4}''$ vertical wall that surrounds half of this $7\frac{3}{4}''$—diameter plate. The entry wall is $\frac{1}{2}''$ at the lowest point and gradually slopes upward. Constructed of dishwasher-safe (up to 180 degrees) white melamine plastic with nonskid feet on base. Latex-free.

Clip-On Guard:
Makes it easy to adapt standard plates for confident self-feeding. Three hooks securely attach guard to plates $9''$–$11''$ in diameter. Guard curves slightly to aid scooping and keep food on plate. Sturdy, attractive white plastic with light gray specks. Dishwasher safe up to 180 degrees F. Latex-free.

12 oz. Insulated Mug with Lid:
A polypropylene mug with an easy-to-grasp handle. Use for either hot or cold liquids. Lid regulates flow of liquids. Dishwasher safe up to 180 degrees F. Latex free.

Feeding Cup:
Large mouthpiece for intake without dribbling. Hole in mouthpiece is large enough to hold a straw. Autoclavable polypropylene with 4-, 6- and 8-oz. markings. Base is five inches in diameter. Dishwasher safe up to 125 degrees F. Base and extra lids sold separately. Latex free.

Transparent Mug with Two Handles:
Clear, high-strength plastic with dual handles for a secure grip. Wide base helps prevent tipping. 10-oz. capacity. White spouted lid. Dishwasher safe up to 125 degrees F. Latex free.

Deluxe Versatilt Table:
For home or clinic, this attractively designed table of tubular steel construction serves many purposes. Useful as a stand for TV, home computer, or typewriter, it is also ideal as an overbed table. Supports 40 to 50 lbs. when in the lowest position. Wood-grained, melamine laminated top has raised edge to keep papers, books, or other materials from sliding off. Can be easily titled to two angles in either direction using the tilt release lever. Easy to assemble. Latex-free.
    *Height adjusts: 25¾" to 39"
    *Surface: 24" L x 14" W x ¾" D
    *Weight: 22 lbs.

Card Rack:
Walnut-stained fiberboard card rack holds all the cards needed for any game. Grooves are slanted and rack is tiered for good visibility. Measures 9½" L x 5" W. Latex-free.

Giant-Face Playing Cards:
Enlarged faces and print on these standard-size playing cards enable those with visual impairments to enjoy card games. Latex-free.

Talking Calculator with Clock/Alarm:
Enter the numbers you wish to calculate, and this calculator will speak the answer. Includes repeat option and adjustable volume. Eight-digit

calculator with memory also has a large LCD display. Alarm clock displays time with hour, minute, and second. Requires 2 AAA batteries (not included). 3½″ W x 5⅛″ L x ¾″ D. Latex-free.

Tek Partner Universal Remote:

Replaces up to four standard remotes and can be used with any combination of TVs, VCRs, and cable boxes. Touch-sensitive lighted keypad lets user operate in the dark. Large ¾″ buttons and bold easy-to-read characters make remote simple to use. Features code retention for easy programming, will not lose any information during a battery change. Extra large frame makes it difficult to misplace, and easy to grasp. Measures 5½″ W x 8½″ L x 2½″ D. Latex free.

Book Butler:

This reading stand/book holder features two spring-loaded posts/arms that open automatically and lock to hold book flat. Pages slip easily from one arm to the other. Easel back positions Book Butler at 45 degree angle. Will accommodate books from paperbacks to encyclopedias. High-impact polystyrene. Measures 9″ H x 7″ W.

Reading Desk with Storage:

Lightweight, portable, and stores small books, paper, and writing/drawing utensils. Use on lap, bed, table, or wheelchair lap tray. Foam-padded base keeps desk from slipping. Tilts to 10 positions. Bottom ledge holds pencils, pens, paper, etc. Work surface is 10½″ x 19″. Folds to 2″ thick. Made of high-strength polystyrene plastic. Latex-free.

Adjustable Folding Table:

Ideal for wheelchair, graduated table or bedside use. Hardwood desktop with easel adjustment provides easy positioning. Built-in handles assist carrying. Folds flat for storage. Measures 14″ W x 17″ L. Latex-free.

Wanchik's Writer Instruments:

Plastic-covered aluminum hand and hand/wrist orthoses hug the palm and hold the index finger to give individuals with weakened hand, finger and/or wrist dexterity the support and control needed to write. Designed to fit pencils and thin ball-points, these writers are easy to slip on and off. Just bend for a customized fit. Latex-free.

Pen/Pencil and Utensil Grips:

Soft grips slip easily onto standard round or hexagonal pencils and most ballpoint pens. Grips form a cushion for the fingers, providing a more efficient, natural, and comfortable hold. Assorted colors. Latex-free.

DIALOGUE RC-200 Hands-Free Telephone:

This telephone enables those with limited mobility—such as quadripleg-ic's and ALS clients—to make and answer telephone calls. Its features include: Voice-activated answering, large nonslip keypad buttons, voice mail/unanswered call indicator, battery backup, automatic scanning and dialing of 20 telephone numbers stored in memory, wireless remote control of all phone functions up to 40 feet away. User can participate in crisp, clear hands-free conversations from up to 15 feet away from phone. Other features include easy access for assistance or emergency help. An optional *AirSwitch* enables user to place and answer telephone calls, plus control every function of the DIALOGUE RC-200 telephone by simply blowing on its air sensor. This device plugs into the telephone's console or remote control. The hands-free telephone can be installed on most surfaces—on a desktop, wheelchair, wall, and more.

Ergo 2000 Adjustable Keyboard:

Recent research has suggested that adjustable split keyboard design may improve postural comfort and reduce user fatigue. This keyboard was designed to allow more comfortable hand positions. You can even sepa-rate the keyboard and place your mouse between each unit. Features mechanical tactile keys. Full IBM compatibility with 286 MHz, 386 MHz, 486 MHz, and Pentium processor-based computer systems. Optional MAC adaptor available by special order. Latex-free.

Wrist-Guide Support:

Wrist Guide foam pad provides proper alignment of hands and wrists with the keyboard. Rises 1″ above the bottom of the keyboard, allowing hands and wrists to remain level. Foam insert included to raise wrists to a 1 degree incline. Wrist Guide folds open and slides easily under key-board. Measures 19″ wide. Latex free.

Ergonomics for Therapists:

Designed as a reference source for therapists interested in tools, tech-niques and a general overview of ergonomics. Written by Karen Jacobs,

Ed.D., OTR/L, CPE, FAOTA, and Carl Bettencourt, OTR/L. 252 pages. Hardcover.

Computer Resources for People with Disabilities:
An up-to-date guide that helps the user evaluate mainstream and assistive technology needs. Soft cover. 284 pages.

Big Red Switch:
When connected to electric or battery-operated devices, this bright red, 5″ diameter switch enables children or people with limited motor function to activate them easily. Entire surface is responsive to less than 3 oz. of pressure and has a low (less than 1½″) profile. Shatterproof plastic construction. Standard 1/8″ (3.5 mm) plug.
    Contains natural rubber latex.

Soft Switch:
Foam-padded switch absorbs shock to lessen impact of those with gross motor difficulties. Velvet cover removes easily for washing. Requires 28-oz. force to activate. Can be mounted with hook and loop (not included), if needed. Red.

The above items may be purchased from:
    Sammons Preston
    An Ability One Company
    P.O. Box 5071
    Bolingbrook, IL 60440-5071
    Phone: 1-800-323-5547
    Fax: 1-800-547-4333
    TDD: 1-800-325-1745

CHAPTER 8

Joining the Work Force

How successfully a disabled individual fits into the work force depends upon several factors. Two factors that must be considered are how well the individual is trained or educated for a given job, and how well he psychologically interacts with nondisabled people. Both of these factors are of paramount importance to corporate America.

Corporate America does question whether disabled individuals are psychologically prepared to interact with nondisabled coworkers. They automatically assume that the disabled individual is not adequately equipped. Financially, corporate America cannot afford to deal with disabled individuals who might curtail their productivity.

The disabled individual is unsophisticated and naive when it comes to fulfilling a role in the work force. He is not as prepared as the average person. He has probably not been vocationally counseled to make him so. Lacking vocational expertise in many areas is frightening. The more intelligent the individual, the more frightened he becomes. All at once, it is obvious that he lacks information about many vocational areas. If the individual has lived an isolated existence until this time, he has no idea what is required of various jobs. For example, he may not know that to be a clerk in a store also requires that he be able to use a cash register. Should he have poor coordination in his hands, he would have difficulty punching in the prices of products. It may come as a surprise to him that being a stock boy requires climbing up a ladder to reach the higher shelves. If the individual has even minor standing, or walking difficulties this would not be a safe job for him.

Problems arise when the disabled individual puts on a false-capability act. He is only fooling himself when he tries to persuade others that he is more able to do a job than he actually may be. It does not take long for those around him to discover this flaw. By insisting that he is more capable than he is, the individual can cause dissension on a job. Both the employer and coworkers become irritated with the disabled individual's grandiose acts. This does not necessarily mean that every disabled individual will create such dissension. The individual who may cause a disturbance on the job likely has social and emotional problems. Joining the work force may be his first experience out on his own. Therefore, it is quite natural for him to flounder when he is turned out into the mainstream.

When the disabled individual realizes he is not equipped to compete with nondisabled peers he may run for the shelter of his home. Other disabled individuals may react in an opposite manner. To hide their feelings of fright, they may exhibit hostility, uncontrolled anger, and act aggressively. It is this type of behavior that causes problems in the work force. Coworkers do not know how to handle these attitudes. In their eyes this is strange behavior. The only solution they see is to isolate themselves from the disabled coworker.

It is not the individual's disability that causes the tension between the two workers. It is the physically disabled individual's adverse personality behavior that triggers dissension in the worker relationship. As one nondisabled worker put it, "His poor speech and the fact that he was in a wheelchair did not bother me at all. What really bothered me was how uncertain he felt about doing his job and how he asked me to do parts of it for him so he could get it done. I did not know what to say to him. I had my own work to get done."

The Giant Transition

Leaving the protection of a home environment and entering the unprotected environment of the work force is one of the hardest steps the physically disabled individual will take in life. Regardless, he must make it if he wishes to become a productive individual. For him to be satisfied to remain at home will result in his amounting to nothing in life. His experiences with society will be limited and his intellectual intake will be limited as well. Emotionally and socially he may exhibit retarded behavior.

It takes a lot of stamina to make the transition from his home environment into his community environment. Nonetheless, he must. No one else can do it for him. He is the only one who knows what it is like to be disabled. Many people may offer to assist in this transition, but it is he who must have the final say as to how he will do it. It is his life which is involved, not the life of friends or even parents and siblings. The individual must grab the reins and become director of his own life.

As he leaves his home environment, the physically disabled individual will experience times when he might want to run back home. He must learn how to handle impending feelings of fright and loneliness. He cannot afford to nurture them in any way. He must begin to run his own life and make his own decisions.

The physically disabled individual who can weather feelings and periods of uncertainty is the individual who will succeed in life. He will learn that feelings of fright and anguish will gain him very little. People in society do not understand that the disabled individual can continually experience such feelings. Nor do they want to know about them. It is up to the disabled individual to handle the impact of his feelings without imposing them on his coworkers.

The physically disabled individual who conquers the impact of disturbing feelings will become a much stronger individual and gain respect from others. He has the capacity to do this regardless of the type or severity of his disability. If he has the intellect and the fortitude to make the transition from the protection of home to a non-protected environment, he will succeed in anything he attempts to do in the future.

Facing Realities in the Work Force

Entering the work force can be a traumatic experience for the physically disabled adult. Feelings of uncertainty, and feelings of fear engulf him. If this is the first time away from his home environment, those feelings will not lessen but become more intense. Infringing feelings of self-consciousness pop up. Although it may not be true, it is easy for the individual to feel that everyone is staring.

As mentioned in previous chapters, it is not that the nondisabled person does not want to relate to the disabled person. He does not know how to relate or what to say to him. The physically disabled individual is aware of the nondisabled coworker's uncertainty about him. When the nondisabled person is coached by company authorities on how to handle this circumstance, their relationship has a chance to be amicable. How amicable it becomes is up to the disabled person. It is his responsibility to encourage compatible interaction between himself and his coworkers.

Another truth that must be faced is that the employer always has feelings of uncertainty during the interview with the disabled. Conducting an interview with a disabled individual is not the favorite job of many employers. They are at a loss as to how to handle the interview. They do not want to hurt the disabled individual, nor do they want to give him false hopes.

The basic fact is that although the disabled individual may have excellent credentials it does not guarantee he will be hired. Whether he is hired or not depends upon the interviewer's attitudes toward disabled people. Many disabled individuals are aware of this fact which is why just going for an interview can be a distressing experience. The disabled person never knows how he will be received by an employer. Even though the individual has adequately prepared himself for the interview, gone to it, and felt it went well, he is often told that they will call him in a few days. His feelings of worth are shaken. He feels even worse when five days after the interview he still has not received a call.

The disabled individual can be spared distress when a realistic assessment of his employability is done. It is imperative that his abilities be assessed. To assume that every disabled individual is unemployable is inaccurate. Nor is the assumption that every disabled individual is employable correct. No two disabled individual's employability abilities are the same. Each must be individually evaluated. Potential work habits and his ability to understand a job's requirements should be the determining factors regarding his employability. This assessment should be made before any type of interview takes place.

The employability of the disabled individual is a two-way street. While his comfort on a job certainly should be considered, it is equally important that he understand the job's specific needs. It is important that the disabled individual be able to fulfill the job's requirements. If he cannot easily fulfill the job's requirements, he should not be considered for it.

There are specific requirements that everyone has to adhere to in seeking employment. The physically disabled adult is no different. Those helping him seek employment should take an inventory of what the individual has to offer. Does he demonstrate a sense of self-worth. Can he deal with daily responsibilities and challenges? Can he contribute responsibly to his peer group? Does he have a positive relationship with peers?

How successful an individual is in seeking a job, or on a job, depends if he has been vocationally evaluated. Every prospective employer has a right to know all the particulars about a disabled individual. Does he know what his physical abilities are? Does he know what his physical inabilities are? Is he seeking a job he may have a chance of succeeding in? Or, is he applying for a job he has dreamed about? The employer has a right to truthful answers of these questions. They are also questions the disabled individual must answer truthfully, for his own good. When he can, a successful vocational future is more likely.

Milly is a good example. She had pursued a college degree in psychology even though she had to use a wheelchair and was significantly limited in her care of herself. Academically she had performed above average. Under ordinary circumstances, Milly would have been eligible for a job as a psychologist. However, this was not to happen for her. Physical inabilities hindered her from being active in such a career.

Milly was referred to me as a potential psychology student intern. The college suggested that she fulfill her internship under my supervision. I was aware of Milly's exceptional academic performance in her studies. I was equally aware of her physical inabilities. Milly was prone to having seizures, had a severe speech impediment, and could not take care of herself. My concern was: What would happen if Milly were to have a child in her office who had a seizure? Could Milly easily call on the telephone, or quickly open her office door to call for help? The answer was obviously no. Furthermore, were Milly to have a seizure herself, how could that be handled and by whom?

These stumbling blocks to Milly's employment were not addressed by her college advisers. They had ignored them and permitted Milly to spend four years of college preparing to be a psychologist. When I asked her college advisers why they encouraged her to enter a profession she could not physically function in, they felt that she, like any other college student, had every right to choose what career she would like to pursue. They did not want to infringe upon her personal rights to choose her own career. The college reminded me that the laws of the land stated that an individual, disabled or not, had every right to make his own choice.

Permitting the physically disabled individual to engage in unrealistic vocational planning borders on cruelty to that individual. Certainly, recognition should be given to the individual's human rights. The important fact is that consideration be given also to his realistic rights. Allowing the disabled person to follow his misguided vocational desires is really submitting him to years of continual disappointment. He is condemning himself to frustration, rejection, and poor judgement.

Words such as realism and truthfulness should be at the top of every disabled person's vocational vocabulary. Use of these words can keep him from soul-searing experiences. If the disabled individual is to be vocationally helped, he must be told facts the way they are in his life, not the way he wishes they were. For him to function in a job where his physical inabilities obviously block him from successfully performing is senseless. It can do nothing but destroy his concept of himself.

Milly paid dearly for not being realistically counseled. Her feelings of defeat, disappointment, and depression were devastating. It was devastating for Milly to spend four years of hard work preparing for a career only to find that the four years yielded nothing positive. She would have fared much better had her advisers at least attempted to counsel her to enter a field of study where her physical inabilities would not have prevented her from functioning at her best.

Forgoing the Job of Your Dreams

Like everyone else, the disabled individual dreams of the jobs he would like to have. Like everyone else, he also dreams of making a lot of money. However, his disability can be a factor in preventing either dream from coming true. The fruition of both dreams are solely based on what he can do and what he cannot do. He must face the brutal truth, seeking not what he would like to do, but what he is physically capable of doing. To ignore this fact and attempt to fulfill his dreams can only result in disappointment. The phrase "be realistic" must dominate his judgement. He must apply it directly to himself.

The disabled individual should guard against blaming himself for not finding employment. He must accept the fact that he cannot fulfill his dream job. He needs to find a job he can easily and successfully handle. Nothing is gained if he gives up on himself. Nor should he toy with the idea of living on Welfare or on a measly Social Security check. This is an excuse for the disabled individual not to face the problems that can confront him. He will be further ahead if he concentrates on finding a job that is adaptable to his physical inabilities.

If the disabled individual cannot find a full-time job, but can only find a part-time job, there is nothing wrong with this. At least he is making some amount of personal income. Being financially reimbursed for one's efforts enhances feelings of self-worth. Feelings of importance surge through the body and allow the individual to look down at the job he is doing and know he is doing it well enough to be paid for his efforts. It is not the amount paid that counts the most, but the fact that someone pays for your efforts that counts. This experience, in itself, can have immeasurable benefits for the disabled individual. It can generate feelings of personal worth and encourage independence. Too often it is assumed that because he is disabled he cannot have the normal wish to make something of himself, contribute financially to a household, or at least financially provide for his own needs.

Importance of Self-Control

The corporate world does not adjust well to being railroaded into making job adaptations. Some companies rebel at doing so. Others find ways of avoiding it. Many companies cannot afford to make extensive job adaptations. Making specific job adaptations for a disabled employee usually does not have a place in their budget.

The corporate world has every right to protect itself against any unnecessary expenses. Companies far more likely to hire a disabled employee if job adaptations can be kept at a minimum. If the individual can join the company with little or no fanfare, he is more likely to be hired. The disabled individual who is accompanied by a job coach will have difficulty being welcomed. Adding one more person to a job that calls for one person is not looked upon favorably. Many companies would prefer that they not be considered a training place for a disabled individual.

This is not to mean that the corporate world is unsympathetic to the employment problems of the disabled. They are and have been known to give donations to make such employment possible. The prospective disabled employee must "sell" himself to the corporate world. No one else can do it for him. Unless he accepts this responsibility the employment problems associated with the disabled individual will continue. The corporate world does not the have time nor the inclination to give the prospective disabled employee a job out of sympathy. Time is of the essence where Corporate America is concerned. Every minute lost is a dollar lost.

The physically disabled adult is much further ahead if he attempts to make his own adaptations to a job. For example, should a certain job require that the employee have computer skills, the disabled employee is being realistic if he provides the necessary help he may need to fulfill this job requirement. If he cannot operate a computer keyboard, he should provide the hired help needed to do it for him so he can fulfill the job requirement. If he must allot a portion of his salary for this purpose, it can be money well spent.

Financial Planning Is a Necessity

With careful planning, the retirement years are secure for most people. They have made sufficient salaries to put part of it away in a company retirement program or invest in stocks and bonds. Whichever they choose, a reasonable amount of money is available to live on after the age of sixty-five. This is rarely the case where disabled individuals are concerned. Even though they may be employed until the age of sixty-five, it is likely they have not been paid a large enough salary to save any portion of it for retirement. As a result, when the disabled individual reaches sixty-five he has little or nothing to live on.

One reason for the existence of this critical situation is that the disabled individual tends to be naive concerning general financial matters and how they can affect him. He does not realize that he has every right to find out details related to the job he hopes to get. He should ask what salary is being offered. If he finds it is not equal to what would be paid to a nondisabled employee, he should refuse the job. The disabled individual will be hesitant about making such an inquiry. If he has not developed a good opinion of himself, he will find it difficult to ask for the same salary paid to every other employee. In a subservient manner, he will accept any job, regardless of its salary, just to have a job.

The place that the disabled individual holds in any work force is a matter of self-respect. He should not submit to conditions on a job that might degrade him in comparison with his nondisabled counterpart. If the disabled individual can perform a job as well, or even better than a nondisabled person, he should be paid the same salary rate. However, such good self-regard and self-respect is often lacking in the disabled individual. As a result, he finds he may not be able to support himself after the age of sixty-five. Because he has no retirement means to fall back on, the disabled individual has to return to living with his family. This situation is critical and comes as a surprise to many people.

Finding a remedy for the financial problems of the elderly disabled individual is difficult today. Society certainly does not hold the answers. This leaves the families of the disabled responsible for their elderly care. Unfortunately, if a family is unable to provide such care, the only alternative for the individual is to reside in a nursing home, a group home, or alone on a small Social Security disability check. Such a future can be humiliating to the disabled individual.

The United States Government and others must consider providing a financial resource for the elderly disabled. Perhaps the federal government might consider establishing an IRA type of account for elderly disabled individuals, sixty-five years and older. Possibilities are presently under consideration under different committees of the Federal Labor Department. If such financial resources could be provided two problems could be solved. It would not only help the disabled person but also help the country. Currently it does nothing but raise everybody's taxes.

In the meantime, there are several ways families might assist in solving this problem. For instance, setting up an IRA account might be considered. Setting aside $500 to $1,000 a year over a specific period of time might result in adequate money for the disabled to retire. Educating families to the financial need of the elderly disabled adult should be given top consideration. This is particularly true today since so many disabled individuals outlive sixty-five years. The answer does not lie in putting these individuals in nursing homes or allowing them to exist on barely nothing.

Rosa's family suggests a way other families can be instrumental in finding a solution. Rosa's family did not have the means to set up an IRA account for her. However, they were sensitive enough to their daughter's feelings to know that as retirement time came for her she had reason to feel apprehensive.

Rosa's case presents a positive outcome. Having to spend her life in a wheelchair limited some of her physical abilities. Nevertheless, she had successfully completed four years of college. Since her major physical limitation was an inability to walk, becoming a secretary had few problems for her. She was skilled at using a typewriter and a computer keyboard. Her telephone etiquette was unflawed. However, Rosa was underpaid. She did not make enough in salary to set aside money for retirement purposes.

When Rosa's family found out she would not receive retirement benefits, everybody in her family started to plan for her future. Her father decided that after he retired he would use some savings to add to the sale of their home and buy a home for Rosa in Florida that would be accessible for her needs. The only stipulation placed on it was that she allow her parents to live with her until they passed on.

The brothers offered no resistance to the plan. One brother accepted the responsibility for paying utility bills and any excess medical bills, a second brother chose to pay the insurance premiums on the house, and the third brother agreed to pay the taxes. Rosa's responsibility was to pay her grocery bill and buy personal items with her monthly disability check.

Everyone in Rosa's family benefited. No one single member was burdened totally with her care. Nor was Rosa abandoned by her family. The arrangement set up by her parents assured Rosa that she could feel secure the rest of her life. Also, her dignity was preserved and her sense of independence was not curtailed. The fact that she had no reason to feel obligated to anyone also helped. Rosa still could be in charge of her own life. Her brothers could live their lives without feeling obligated to look after her daily. Rosa had her life, her brothers had theirs. Neither interfered with the other.

Rosa is a good example of how a critical time in the life of a disabled person can be turned into a stable future. Everyone in the family benefits. Just because one member has a disability is no reason for him to give up living and be put in a nursing home. Yet, this is what happens in many cases. The dignity and the humanistic part of the disabled person is not honored. Family members often become obsessed with getting free from any care and responsibility of the disabled individual. In some instances it is the disabled person's family who reject him more than society does.

Needed! A Health-Care Program for the Disabled

A health-care program specifically designed to cover the growing disabled population is in dire need. There is no doubt that if such a program was available to corporations in this country, the employability of the disabled individual might be far more generally accepted. Presently disabled employees are being dropped by companies' managed care programs. Corporations are forced to do this because covering many of the medical needs of the disabled employee can significantly raise the insurance premiums of the nondisabled employees.

The medical profession must be made to understand that to be a disabled person, or to care for such a person, involves considerable ongoing financial expenses. These expenses can include medications, therapy sessions, rehabilitation equipment, and in some instances private education and private care. Few family budgets can handle these expenses. Yet, many health-care plans being considered by the government are not designed to include chronic care of the disabled. Thus, families and disabled individuals have nowhere to turn for needed rehabilitation care.

Wendy was a victim of her employer's insurance provider. In a matter of minutes Wendy went from being a junior executive in a big company to being a completely helpless young woman in a wheelchair. While driving to work Wendy's car was struck by another car causing her to become permanently paralyzed from the hips down. In a flash, all of Wendy's dreams of marriage, starting a family, and climbing the corporate ladder vanished. This forced Wendy to turn her thoughts toward self-survival.

The intense rehabilitation therapy necessary to bring Wendy's physical agility back was expensive. Learning to function physically within a paralyzed body resulted in her becoming depressed. Feelings of insecurity grew. The insurance company's denial of long-term rehabilitation coverage and eventual cancellation of her policy did not help Wendy's outlook on life. Her extensive rehabilitation needs were cited as a medical risk to the insurance company. Upon disclosure of their decision, the hospital she was in informed Wendy that her insurance would no longer cover her care and rehabilitation costs.

Wendy is one of many cases I have handled in my practice. I have evaluated numerous disabled individuals of all ages and from all socio-economic strata. During the years I have become painfully aware of the blatantly inadequate health-care program for disabled individuals, particularly for young children.

Prosthetics, G-tube feeders, kidney transplants, and long-term rehabilitation therapies are medical necessities that many disabled individuals cannot exist without. To offer any type of comprehensive health care plan that reduces or eliminates altogether benefits for chronically disabling conditions is a blatant form of discrimination. It is, in essence, condemning the innocent.

Under many medical plans, rehabilitation services such as physical, occupational, and speech therapies as well as psychological evaluations and counseling are limited to only sixty days insurance coverage. This unrealistic short-term program does nothing for the majority of disabled individuals. It is not likely that any disabling condition can even be helped in a matter of sixty days. Most disabling conditions require months and even years of treatment. Rarely is anything accomplished for the individual in less time.

Unfortunately medical care and services for the disabled are becoming more difficult and costly to obtain. Physicians offering such care feel their best medical judgements are usurped by policies of HMO and managed health care providers. For example, if a rehabilitation specialist prescribes a specific regime of therapy to benefit a patient, payment for these services is determined by nonmedical "bureaucrats" that arbitrarily decide how much therapy a given patient is to receive, and how much he needs.

Paula, who at eighteen months of age had a chronic heart condition that resulted in two disabling strokes, is an example of how HMOs interfere in prescribed treatment programs. Following heart and brain surgery, Paula's doctor prescribed lengthy therapy. Nevertheless, the insurance company would not honor Paula's doctor requirement. They would only cover sixty therapeutic sessions. This was in spite of the fact that after fifty-five sessions, Paula did begin to show improvement. She was able to take a few steps in a walker, proving that continued therapy could benefit her. However, this progress failed to impress HMO officials. The insurance coverage was terminated following the authorized sixty therapy sessions.

It is crucial that rehabilitation services essential to the disabled individual's well-being be recognized by HMO administrators and their managed health-care counterparts. If they are not, millions of Americans will be prevented from reaching their maximum vocational level and, thus will require continuous support from the American taxpayer. This makes it imperative that disabled people have a health care policy designed to meet their individual needs. This need must be addressed by the government as a matter of simple justice, moral urgency, and good long-range economic sense.

Two-year-old Cindy is another case in point. She had a chronic kidney-liver disease. Her mother was overwhelmed by medication costs of $200 per week. If a kidney transplant was going to be necessary, the family could not privately finance it. Their budget would not cover such an expense. "Our insurance company has notified us that they will no longer cover our child's needs," her mother grieved. "What are we supposed to do? Let her die?"

Every parent caring for a disabled child goes through a grieving process. Whether the child is born cerebral palsied, diagnosed with muscular dystrophy, or disabled as a result of an accident, the emotional trauma to the parent is the same. The parents must cope with feelings of loss, agony, uncertainty, grief and depression as they come to terms with the new responsibility of caring for a disabled child. This is true whether the child is two years old or eighteen.

"Our eighteen year old daughter has a traumatic head injury resulting from an automobile accident," agonize her parents. "She has to be fed liquid nourishment through a G-tube. The cost for this is $85 a case, which covers only for four days of feedings. We have recently been notified that our insurance company will no longer cover our daughter's needs." This forced the family to sign their daughter up with the state's Medicaid program, which also had its faults: it could not cover the costs of her daily feedings.

Stringent insurance and HMO policies can be detrimental to the health of a disabled person. When HMOs or managed-health care providers only allow a child three or four visits to a therapist per month, that child's physical development suffers. The child is not given the opportunity to develop to his maximum. Limiting of services is also noticeable when a child needs special rehabilitation aids. A case in point is the child who must wear special shoes, or who must walk in braces. As he grows older and outgrows the shoes or braces it will be necessary to purchase new ones. Few family budgets can stand such continuous expense. Special shoes can cost over $100 and braces can cost anywhere from $1,000 to $2,200. The same is true of the child who must use a wheelchair. As he grows older, he will need a larger chair which can cost thousands of dollars.

It must be recognized that those individuals whose lives are supported by extraordinary rehabilitative measures, including round-the-clock care and tube-induced feedings, have as much right to adequate medical coverage as any other citizen. Medical knowledge, technology, and rehabilitation services are capable of providing such benefit, but not without time and cost. It is crucial that rehabilitation services essential to the disabled individual's well-being be recognized by HMO administrators and their managed health-care counterparts. If they are not, millions of Americans will be prevented from reaching their maximum vocational level and, thus, will require continuous support from the taxpayer.

Disabled children and adults do not deserve to live without a health care policy designed specifically to their needs. The necessity of meeting such needs must be recognized by society as a matter of simple justice, moral urgency, and good long-term economic sense.

Who Determines the Disabled Person's Future?

Those in federal government, and the corporate world as well as physicians, physical medicine specialists, and psychologists determine whether the future for disabled individuals will be positive or negative. However, they cannot do it totally alone. The disabled individual himself must accept some responsibility.

Before a productive future can materialize, several issues must be addressed. One of the more recent ones is The Americans with Disabilities Act (ADA). Although this Act became law in 1990, it is limited in scope and service. The consensus of opinion is that it needs to be redefined and its purpose better clarified. For example, the Act states that it serves all types of disabled individuals. To many this is misleading. The act does not provide coverage for many individuals who are severely involved. The law would be considered more accurate if ADA individually classified the different types of disabilities as to their specific limitations and needs, accordingly. A person with a heart condition should not be put into the same classification as the person who is so severely involved, physically, that he needs assistance to basically function. Most people with heart conditions usually can physically function on the job as easily as any non-disabled worker.

Equal criticism must be made regarding the various state rehabilitation offices. Although these offices provide the means for disabled individuals either to attend college or otherwise receive specialized training, this gesture loses its importance if the individual cannot find employment. This realization can be emotionally devastating. It forces the individual to look at himself and realize how limited his physical abilities are. This makes it imperative for the disabled individual to receive vocational counseling before he is placed in the workforce, or is encouraged to seek employment.

Fifty years ago I could have been an employment casualty. Because my father was intent upon me becoming a physician, I went off to college determined to someday become a doctor and make a lot of money. It never occurred to me that a medical school would not admit me. Fortunately, in my freshman year of college, my professors had other ideas for me. They questioned whether I would be admitted to a medical school. I remember resenting this counsel. Nevertheless, when I was ready to listen, the professors encouraged me to study for a career that would make the best use of the undamaged part of my body, namely my brain. Thus I studied for a career in psychology.

I am eternally grateful to those professors who dared to infringe upon my rights as an individual and candidly counsel me. Professors today hesitate doing this for disabled college students. Rather, they honor their rights and let them continue whatever line of study they wish, no matter the consequences. I owe my success to my professors' persistence in forcing me see reality as it was and not as I wanted it to be. Had they not done this, I would have gone through medical school and probably done fairly well in my studies. When it came time to be accepted for a residency appointment or go into practice, I would have had to face the fact that my years of study in medical school had been for naught.

It is hoped that in the new millennium the federal government will provide a variety of additional services for disabled individuals. For example, they should be alert to the fact that disabled individuals now live longer and that, like their nondisabled counterparts, can hold jobs until they are sixty-five years old. This emphasizes the need for the creation of a retirement program for disabled individuals. Many cannot provide this for themselves because they are often not paid a big enough salary to set aside funds for retirement. The brutal fact is that while employment is important and essential to the disabled individual's lifestyle and should thus be pursued, it means nothing if at the time of his retirement he has nothing to live on but a small Social Security check.

With the advent of new technology, it is hoped that the lifestyle of the disabled individual will improve. But first, society must realize the "normal aspects" that make up a disabled individual's personality. Only then can positive steps be taken into the future. Much will be gained when it is realized that there is no such thing as a disabled heart or disabled soul.

Appendixes

State Vocational Resources

Alabama
Alabama Department of
Rehabilitation Services
2129 East South Boulevard
Montgomery, AL 36111-0586
334-281-8780
Toll free in AL: 1-800-441-7607
TDD: 334-613-2249
Fax: 334-281-1973
Website: www.rehab.state.al.us

Alaska
Division of Vocational Rehabilitation
Goldbelt Building, 1st Floor
801 West 10th Street, Suite A
Juneau, AK 99801-1894
907-465-2814
Toll free in AK: 1-800-478-2815
TDD: 907-465-2814
Fax: 907-465-2856
Website: www.labor.state.ak.us/dvr

Arizona
Rehabilitation Services Administration
1789 West Jefferson

2nd Floor, NW
Phoenix, AZ 85007
602-542-3332
Toll free: 1-800-563-1221
TDD: 602-542-6049
Fax: 602-542-3778
Website: www.azrsa.org

Arkansas
Arkansas Rehabilitation Services, Arkansas
   Department of Workforce
P.O. Box 3781
1616 Brookwood Drive
Little Rock, AR 72203
501-296-1616
Toll free in AR: 1-800-330-0631
TDD: 501-296-1669
Fax: 501-296-1655
Website: www.state.ar.us/ars/ars2.html

California
Department of Rehabilitation
2000 Evergreen Street
Sacramento, CA 95815
916-263-7365

TDD: 916-263-7477
Fax: 916-263-7474
Website: www.rehab.ca.gov

Colorado
Division of Vocational Rehabilitation
Administration Office
2211 West Evans, Building B
Denver, Colorado 80223
720-884-1234
Fax 720-884-1213
Website: www.state.co.us

Connecticut
Division of Client Services
State Department of Social Services
Bureau of Rehabilitation Services
25 Sigourney Street
Hartford, CT 06106
860-424-4848
Fax: 860-424-4850

Delaware
Division of Vocational Rehabilitation
Department of Labor
4425 North Market Street; P.O. Box 9969
Wilmington, DE 19809-0969
302-761-8275
TDD: 302-761-8336
Fax: 302-761-6611
Website: www.dvr.state.de.us

District of Columbia
Rehabilitation Services Administration
Department of Human Services
810 First Street, NE; 10th Floor
Washington, DC 20002
202-442-8663
Fax: 202-442-8742

Florida
Division of Vocational Rehabilitation
Department of Labor and Employment
    Security
2002 Old St. Augustine Road
Building A
Tallahassee, FL 32399-0696
850-488-6210
TDD: 850-488-0059
Fax: 850-488-8062
Website: www.fdles.state.fl.us

Georgia
Division of Rehabilitation Services
Department of Human Resources
2 Peachtree Street, NW
35th Floor
Atlanta, GA 30303-3142
404-657-3000
Fax: 404-657-3079
Website: www.vocrehabga.org

Hawaii
Division of Vocational Rehabilitation and
Services for the Blind
Department of Human Services
601 Kamokila Blvd.
Room 515
Honolulu, HI 96707
808-692-7719
808-692-7718
Fax: 808-692-7727

Idaho
Division of Vocational Rehabilitation
650 West State
P.O. Box 83720
Boise, ID 83720-0096
208-334-3390
Toll free in ID: 1-800-856-2720
TDD: 208-334-3390
Fax: 208-334-5305
Website: www.state.id.us/idvr/idvrhome/

Illinois
Department of Human Services
Office of Rehabilitation Services
623 East Adams Street
PO Box 19429
Springfield, IL 62794-9429
217-782-2094
Toll free in IL: 1-800-843-6154
TDD: 217-782-5734;
Fax: 217-785-5753

Indiana
Bureau of Aging and In-home Services
402 West Washington Street
Room W-454
P.O. Box 7083
Indianapolis, IN 46207-7083
317-232-7020
Toll free: 1-800-457-8283

TDD toll free in IN: 1-800-545-7763
Fax: 317-232-7867

Iowa
Department of Education
Division of Vocational Rehabilitation
    Services
510 East 12th Street
Des Moines, IA 50319
515-281-6731
Toll free in IA: 1-800-532-1486
TTD/TTY: 1-515-281-4211
Fax: 515-281-4703
Website: www.dvrs.state.ia.us

Kansas
Rehabilitation Services
Department of Social and Rehabilitation
    Services
3640 SW Topeka Blvd
Suite 150
300 SW Oakley
Topeka, KS 66611
785-296-2500
TDD: 785-267-0352
Fax: 785-267-0263
Website: www.ink.org/public/srs

Kentucky
Department of Vocational Rehabilitation
209 St. Clair
Frankfort, KY 40601
502-564-4440
Toll free in KY: 1-800-372-7172
TDD toll free: 1-888-420-9874
Fax: 502-564-6745

Louisiana
Louisiana Rehabilitation Services
Department of Social Services
8225 Florida Blvd.
Baton Rouge, LA 70806-4834
225-925-4131
Toll free in LA: 1-800-737-2958
TDD: 225-295-8900
Fax: 225-925-4184
Website: www.dss.state.la.us

Maine
Bureau of Rehabilitation
Department of Labor

150 State House Station
Augusta, ME 04333-0150
207-287-5100
Toll free in ME: 1-800-332-1003
Toll free: 1-800-698-4440 (National)
TTY: 207-287-5146
Fax: 207-287-5133

Maryland
Division of Rehabilitation Services
State Department of Education
2301 Argonne Drive
Baltimore, MD 21218
410-554-9388
Toll free in MD: 1-888-554-0334
Fax: 410-554-9412
Website: www.dors.state.md.us/

Massachusetts
Massachusetts Rehabilitation Commission
Fort Point Place
27-43 Wormwood Street
Boston, MA 02210
617-727-2183
Toll free in MA: 1-800-245-6543
TDD: 617-204-3868
Fax: 617-727-1354
Website: www.state.ma.us/mrc

Michigan
Michigan Rehabilitation Services
Michigan Department of Career
    Development
P.O. Box 30010
Lansing, MI 48909
517-373-3390
517-335-2221
Toll free in MI: 1-800-605-6722
TDD toll free: 1-888-605-6722
Fax: 517-373-0565
Website: www.mrs.state.mi.us

Disability Determination Service
Family Independence Agency
P.O. Box 30011
Lansing, MI 48909
517-373-7830
Toll free in MI: 1-800-366-3404
Fax: 517-373-2149

Minnesota
Rehabilitation Services Branch
Department of Economic and Security
390 North Robert Street
5th Floor
St. Paul, MN 55101
651-296-5616
TDD: 612-296-3900
Fax: 651-297-5159
Website: www.des.state.mn.us

Mississippi
Department of Rehabilitation Services
P.O. Box 51
Madison, MS 39110
601-853-5100
Toll free in MS: 1-800-962-2230
Toll free: 1-800-443-1000 (National)
Fax: 601-853-5205
Website: www.mdrs.state ms.us

Missouri
Division of Vocational Rehabilitation
State Department of Education
3024 West Truman Blvd.
Jefferson City, MO 65109
573-751-3251 573-751-3901
Fax: 573-751-1441
Website: services.dese.state.mo.us

Montana
Disability Services Division
Dept. of Public Health and Human Services
P.O. Box 4210
Helena, MT 59604-4210
406-444-2590
TDD: 406-444-2590
Fax: 406-444-3632
Website: www.dphhs.mt.gov

Nebraska
Div. of Vocational Rehabilitation Services
State Department of Education
P.O. Box 94987
Lincoln, NE 68509
402-471-3649
Toll free in NE: 1-877-637-3422
TDD: 402-471-3659
Fax: 402-471-0788
Website: www.vocrehab.state.ne.us

Nevada
Nevada Rehabilitation Division
505 East King Street; Room 502
Carson City, NV 89701-3705
775-684-4075 775-684-4040
TDD: 775-684-8400
Fax: 775-684-4184
Website: www.state.nv.us

New Hampshire
Division of Adult Learning and
    Rehabilitation
78 Regional Drive; Building 2
Concord, NH 03301
603-271-3471
Fax: 603-271-7095

New Jersey
Div. of Vocational Rehabilitation Services
135 East State Street; PO Box 398
Trenton, NJ 08625-0398
609-292-5987
TDD: 609-292-2919
Fax: 609-292-8347

New Mexico
Division of Vocational Rehabilitation
Department of Education
435 St. Michaels Drive, Building D
Santa Fe, NM 87505
505-954-8500
TDD: 505-954-8500
Fax: 505-954-8562
Website: www.state.nm.us/dvr

New York
Office of Vocational and Educational Services
    for Individuals with Disabilities
New York State Education Department
One Commerce Plaza; Room 1606
Albany, NY 12234
518-474-2714
TDD: 518-486-3773
Fax: 518-474-8802

North Carolina
Div. of Vocational Rehabilitation Services
Department of Health and Human Services
2801 Mail Service Center
Raleigh, NC 27699-2801
919-733-3364

TDD: 919-733-5924
Fax: 919-733-7968

North Dakota
Disability Services Division
Department of Human Services
Dacotah Foundation Bldg.
600 South Second Street
Suite 1B
Bismarck, ND 58504-5729
701-328-8950 Toll free in ND: 1-800-755-
2745
TDD: 701-328-8969

Ohio
Rehabilitation Services Commission
400 East Campus View Blvd.
Columbus, OH 43235-4604
614-438-1210
Toll free in OH: 1-800-282-4536
TDD: 614-438-1334
Fax: 614-438-1257
Website: www.state.oh.us/rsc

Oklahoma
Department of Rehabilitation Services
3535 NW 58th St.
Suite 500
Oklahoma City, OK 73112
405-951-3400
Toll free: 1-800-845-8476
TDD: 405-951-3400; Toll free: 1-800-845-
8476
Fax: 405-951-3529
Website: www.onenet/~drspiowm

Oregon
Division of Vocational Rehabilitation
Department of Human Resources
Human Resources Building
500 Summer St., NE
Salem, OR 97310-1018
503-945-5880
Toll free: 1-877-277-0513 (Nat'l)
TDD: 503-945-5894
Fax: 503-947-5025
Website: www.vrdweb.hr.state.or.us

Pennsylvania
Office of Vocational Rehabilitation
Labor and Industry Building

7th and Forster Streets
Harrisburg, PA 17120
717-787-5244
Toll free in PA: 1-800-442-6351
TDD: 717-783-8917
Fax: 651-297-5159
Website: www.des.state.pa.us

Rhode Island
Division of Community Services
Office of Rehabilitation Services
Department of Human Services
40 Fountain Street
Providence, RI 02903-1898
401-421-7005
Toll free in RI: 1-800-752-8088
TDD: 401-421-7016
Fax: 401-421-9259
Website: www.ors.state.ri.us

South Carolina
Vocational Rehabilitation Department
1410 Boston Avenue
P.O. Box 15
West Columbia, SC 29171-0015
803-896-6504
TDD: 803-896-6635
Fax: 803-896-6529
Website: www.scvrd.net

South Dakota
Division of Rehabilitation Services
Department of Human Services
East Highway 34; Hillsview Plaza
c/o 500 East Capitol
Pierre, SD 57501-5070
605-773-3195
TDD: 605-773-5990
Fax: 605-773-5483
Website: www.state.sd.us/dhs/drs/welcome3

Tennessee
Rehabilitation Services
Department of Human Services
Citizens Plaza State Office Bldg.
400 Deaderick Street, 15th Floor
Nashville, TN 37248-0060
615-313-4714
TDD: 615-313-4714
Fax: 615-741-4165
Website: www.state.tn.us

Texas
Texas Rehabilitation Commission
Central Office; 4900 North Lamar Blvd.
Austin, TX 78751
512-424-4001 512-424-4002
Toll free: 1-800-628-5115
TDD: 512-424-4067
Fax: 512-424-4012
Website: www.rehab.state.tx.us

Utah
Utah State Office of Rehabilitation
250 East Fifth South
Salt Lake City, UT 84111
Toll free in UT: 1-800-473-7530
TDD: 801-538-7530
Fax: 801-538-7522
Website: www.usor.state.ut.us

Vermont
Vocational Rehabilitation Division
103 South Main Street
Waterbury, VT 05671-2303
Fax: 802-241-3359

Virginia
Department of Rehabilitative Services
8004 Franklin Farms Drive
P.O. Box K-300
Richmond, VA 23288-0300
804-662-7010 Toll free in VA:
    1-800-552-5019
TDD: 804-662-9040
Fax: 804-662-9532

Washington
Division of Vocational Rehabilitation
Department of Social and Health Services
P.O. Box 45340

Olympia, WA 98504-5340
360-438-8000
Toll free in WA: 1-800-637-5627
TDD: 360-438-8000
Fax: 360-438-8007
Website: www.wa.gov/dshs/dvr

West Virginia
Division of Rehabilitation Services
State Capitol Complex
P.O. Box 50890
Charleston, WV 25305-0890
304-766-4601
Toll free in WV: 1-800-642-8207
TDD: 304-766-4965
Fax: 304-766-4905
Website: www.wvdrs.org

Wisconsin
Division of Vocational Rehabilitation
Department of Workforce Development
2917 International Lane, 3rd Floor
P.O. Box 7852
Madison, WI 53707-7852
608-243-5600
Toll free: 1-800-442-3477 (Nat'l)
TDD: 608-243-5601
Fax: 608-243-5680
Website: www.dwd.dvr.state.wi.us

Wyoming
Wyoming Department of Employment
Vocational Rehabilitation
1100 Herschler Building
1st Floor East
Cheyenne, WY 82002
307-777-7389
TDD: 307-777-7389
Fax: 307-777-5939

Educational Financial Aid by State

Alabama
Alabama Commission on Higher
    Education
PO Box 302000
Montgomery, AL 36130
334-242-1998

Alaska
Alaska Commission on Higher
    Education
3030 Vintage Blvd.
Juneau, AK 99801-7109
907-465-2962 or 800-441-2962

Fax 907-465-5316
Website: www.state.ak.us

Arizona
Arizona Commission for Postsecondary
    Education
2020 N Central Ave
Suite. 275
Phoenix, AZ 85004-4503
602-229-2591
Fax 602-229-259
Website: www.acpe.asu.edu

Arkansas
Arkansas Dept. of Higher Education
Financial Aid Division
114 East Capitol Avenue
Little Rock, AR 72201-3818
501-324-9300 or 800-54-STUDY
Fax 501-371-2001
Website: www.state.ar.us/kids_edu

California
California Student Aid Commission
PO Box 419027
Rancho Cordova, CA 95741-9027
916-445-0880

Colorado
Colorado Commission on Higher Education
1300 Broadway
2nd floor
Denver, CO 80203
303-866-2723
Fax 303-860-9750
Website: www.state.co.us

Connecticut
Connecticut State Dept. of Higher Education
Office of Student Financial Assistance
61 Woodland St.
Hartford, CT 06105-2391
860-974-1855
Fax 860-974-1311
Website: www.ctdhe.org

Delaware
Delaware Commission on Higher Education
Carvel State Office Bldg.
820 N French St.
5th floor
Wilmington, DE 19801

302-577-3240
Website: www.doe.state.de.us/high-ed

Florida
Florida Dept. of Education
Bureau of Student Financial Assistance
325 West Gaines Street
124 Collins Building
Tallahassee, FL 32399
888-827-2004
Webste: www.firn.edu/doe/bsfa

Georgia
Georgia Student Finance Commission
Scholoarship and Grants Division
2082 E Exchange PL
Suite 100
Tucker, GA 30084-5305
770-414-3000 or 800-776-6878
Fax 770-414-3144
Website: www.gsfc.org

Hawaii
Hawaii State Postsecondary Education
    Commission
Bachman Hall
Room 112
University of Hawaii
2444 Dole St.
Honolulu, HI 96822-2394
808-956-8213

Idaho
Idaho State Board of Education
650 W State St.
Rm.307
PO Box 83720
Boise, ID 83720-0037
208-334-2270
Fax 208-334-2632
Website: www.sde.state.id.us/osbe

Illinois
Illinois Student Assistance Commission
Scholarship and Grants Services
1755 Lake Cook Rd
Deerfield, IL 60015-5209
847-948-8550 or 800-899-ISAC
Website: ssg@isac-online.org

Indiana
State Student Assistance Commission of
    Indiana
ISTA Center Bldg.
150 W Market St., Ste 500
Indianapolis, IN 46204-2811 317-232-2350
Website: www.state.in.us/ssaci

Iowa
Iowa College Student Aid Commission
200 10th St., 4th fl
Des Moines, IA 50309-3609
515-242-3344
Fax 515-242-3388
Website: www.iowacollegeaid.org

Kansas
Kansas Board of Regents
700 SW Harrison St., Ste 1410
Topeka, KS 66603-3760
785-296-3201
Website: www.ksbe.state.ks.us

Kentucky
Kentucky Higher Education Assistance
    Authority
1050 US 127 South
Frankfort, KY 40601-4323
502-696-7381 or 800-928-8926
Fax 502-696-7373
Website: www.kheaa.com

Louisiana
Louisiana Office of Student Financial
    Assistance
PO Box 91202
Baton Rouge, LA 70821-9202
225-922-1011 or 800-259-LOAN
Fax 225-922-0790

Maine
Finance Authority of Maine
Maine Education Assistance Division
1 Weston Ct
State House Station 119
Augusta, ME 04333
207-287-2183

Maryland
Maryland Higher Education Commission
State Scholarship Administration

16 Francis St.
Anapolis, MD 21401-1781
410-974-5370

Massachusetts
Office of Student Financial Assistance
330 Stuart St.
Boston, MA 02116
617-727-9420

Michigan
Michigan Higher Education Assistance
    Authority
Office of Scholarships/Grants
PO Box 30462
Lansing, MI 48909-7962
517-373-3394

Minnesota
Minnesota Higher Education Services Office
Capitol Square Bldg.
550 Cedar St., Ste 400
St. Paul, MN 55101
612-296-3974

Mississippi
Mississippi Office of State Student Financial
    Aid
3825 Ridgewood Rd
Jackson, MS 39221-6453
601-982-6570

Missouri
Missouri Coordinating Board for Higher
    Education
3515 Amazonas Dr
Jefferson City, MO 65109-5717
314-751-2361

Montana
Montana Guaranteed Student Loan Program
2500 Broadway
PO Box 203101
Helena, MT 59620-3101
406-444-6594

Nebraska
Nebraska Department of Education
301 Centennial Mall, South
PO Box 94987

Lincoln, NE 68509-4987
402-471-2295

Nevada
Nevada State Dept. of Education
700 E 5th St.
Carson City, NV 89710
702-687-3100

New Hampshire
New Hampshire Postsecondary Education
  Commission
2 Industrial Park Dr
Concord, NH 03301-8512
603-271-2555

New Jersey
New Jersey Dept. of Higher Education
Office of Student Assistance
4 Quakerbridge Plaza CN 540
Trenton, NJ 08625
609-588-3268

New Mexico
New Mexico Educational Assistance
  Foundation
3900 Osuna Rd, NE; PO Box 27020
Albuquerque, NM 87125-7020
505-345-3371

New York
New York State Higher Education Services
  Corp
Student Information
99 Washington Ave
Albany, NY 12255
518-474-5642

North Carolina
North Carolina State Education Assistance
  Authority
Scholarship/Grant Services
PO Box 2688
Chapel Hill, NC 27515-2688
919-549-8614

North Dakota
North Dakota University System
Student Financial Assistance Program
State Capitol, 10th fl

600 E Blvd.
Bismarck, ND 58505-0230
701-224-4114

Ohio
Ohio Student Aid Commission
State Grants/Scholarships
309 S 4th St.
Columbus, OH 43266-0610
614-466-3091

Oklahoma
Oklahoma State Regents for Higher
  Education
500 Education Bldg.
State Capitol Complex
Oklahoma City, OK 73105-4503
405-524-9100

Oregon
Oregon State Scholarship Commission
1500 Valley River Dr, Ste 100
Eugene, OR 97401
(800) 452-8807

Pennsylvania
Pennsylvania Higher Education Assistance
  Agency
1200 N 7th St.
Harrisburg, PA 17102-1444
717-257-2800

Rhode Island
Rhode Island Higher Education Assistance
  Authority
Scholarship/Grant Division
560 Jefferson Blvd.
Warwick, RI 02886
401-736-1100

South Carolina
South Carolina Commission on Higher
  Education
133 Main St., Ste 200
Columbia, SC 29201
803-737-2277

South Dakota
South Dakota Dept. of Education and
  Cultural Affairs

Office of the Secretary
700 Governors Dr
Pierre, SD 57501-2291
605-773-3134

Tennessee
Tennessee Student Assistance Corp
Parkway Towers
404 James Robertson Pkwy
Suite 1950
Nashville, TN 37243-0820
615-741-1346

Texas
Texas Higher Education Coordinating
  Board
Division of Student Services
PO Box 12788
Capitol Station
Austin, TX 78711-2788
512-483-6340

Utah
Utah State Board of Regents
355 W North Temple
3 Triad Center
Suite 550
Salt Lake City, UT 84180-1205
801-321-7100

Vermont
Vermont Student Assistance Corp
Champlain Mill
PO Box 2000
Winooski, VT 05404-2000
802-654-3765

Virgin Islands
Board of Education
1 Storre Gronne Gade
PO Box 11900
Charlotte Amalie, VI 00801
809-774-4546

Virginia
State Council of Higher Education for
  Virginia

Financial Aid Office
James Monroe Bldg.
101 N 14th St.
Richmond, VA 23219
804-371-7941

Washington
Washington Higher Education Coordinating
  Board
917 Lakeridge Way
PO Box 43430
Olympia, WA 98504-3430
360-753-3571

Washington, D.C.
Office of Postsecondary Education, Research,
  and Assistance
D.C. Dept. of Human Services
2100 Martin Luther King Jr. Ave., SE
Suite 401
Washington, DC 20020-5732
202-727-3688

West Virginia
State College and University Systems
  of WV
Central Office
3110 MacCorkle Ave, SE
PO Box 4007
Charleston, WV 25364-4007
304-347-1266

Wisconsin
Wisconsin Higher Educational Aids Board
131 W Wilson St.
PO Box 7885
Madison, WI 53707-7885
608-267-2206

Wyoming
Wyoming State Dept. of Education
Hathaway Bldg., 2nd fl
2300 Capitol Ave
Cheyenne, WY 82002-0050
307-777-7673

Other Helpful Agencies

American Association for Active Lifestyles and Fitness
1900 Association Drive
Reston, VA 20191
703-476-3400
Fax 703-476-9527
Email aaalf@aahperd.org
Website: www.aahperd.org/aalf.html

American Occupational Therapy Association
4720 Montgomery Lane
P.O. Box 31220
Bethesda, MD 20824
301-652-2682
Fax 301-652-7711
Website: www.aota.org

American Physical Therapy Association
1111 North Fairfax Street
Alexandria, VA 22314-1488
800-999-2782
Fax 703-684-7343
Website: www.apta.org

American Speech-Language-Hearing Association
10801 Rockville Pike
Rockville, MD 20852
800-638-8255
Fax 301-571-0457
Website: www.asha.org

The Compassionate Friends
P.O. Box 3696
Oak Brook, IL 60522-3696
630-990-0010
Fax 630-990-0246
Website: www.compassionatefriends.org

Council For Exceptional Children
1110 North Glebe Road, 3rd Floor
Arlington, VA 22201
Website: www.cec.sped.org

Disabled Sports USA
451 Hungerford Drive
Suite 100
Rockville, MD 20850
301-217-0960
TDD 301-217-0693
Fax 301-217-0968
Website: www.dsusa.org

Federation for Children with Special Needs
1135 Tremont Street
Suite 420
Boston, MA 02120
Voice/TTY 617-236-7210
800-331-0688
Fax 617-572-2094
Website: www.fscn.org

Girl Scouts of the U.S.A.
420 5th Avenue
15th floor Program Group
New York, NY 10018
212-852-8000
Fax 212-852-6515
Website: www.gsusa.org

Independent Living Aids, Inc.
27 East Mall
Plainview, NY 11803
516-752-8080 or 800-537-2118
Fax 516-752-3135
Website: www.independentliving.com

National Association of Private Schools for Exceptional Children
1522 K Street, NW
Suite 1032
Washington, DC 20005
202-408-3340
Fax 202-408-3340
Website: www.napsec.com

National Council on Independent Living
1916 Wilson Boulevard, Suite 2
Arlington, VA 22201
703-525-3406
TTY 703-525-4153

Fax 703-525-3409
Website: www.ncil.org

**National Information Center for Children
and Youth with Disabilities**
P.O. Box 1492
Washington, DC 20013
Voice/TDD 800-695-0285 or 202-884-8200
Fax 202-884-8441
Website: www.nichcy.org

National Organization on Disability
910 16th Street NW, Suite 600
Washington, DC 20006
202-293-5960
TDD 202-293-5968
Fax 202-293-7999
Website: www.nod.org

**Office of Special Education and
Rehabilitative Services**
330 C Street SW
Room 3132
Washington, DC 20202-2524
202-205-8241
TTY 202-205-4208
Fax 202-401-2608
Website: www.ed.gov/OFFICES/OSERS

Sammons Preston Catalog
An Ability One Company
P.O. Box 5071
Bolingbrook, IL 60440-5071
800-323-5547
TDD 800-325-1745
Fax 800-547-4333

Scoliosis Research Society
6300 North River Road, Suite 727

Rosemont, IL 60018-4226
847-698-1627
Fax 847-823-0536
Website: www.srs.org

Sibling Support Project
Children's Hospital and Regional Medical
   Center
P.O. Box 5371/CL-09
Seattle, WA 98105-0371
206-527-5712
Fax 206-527-5705
Website: www.chmc.org/department/
   sibsupp

United Cerebral Palsy Associations
1660 L Street, NW
Suite 700
Washington, DC 20036
800-872-5827
TDD 202-776-0406
Fax 202-776-0414
Website: www.ucp.org

US Access Board
1331 F Street, NW
Suite 1000
Washington, DC 20004-1111
800-872-2253
TTY 800-993-2822 or 202-272-5449

Wheelchair Sports, USA
3593 East Fountain Boulevard
Suite L-1
Colorado Springs, Colorado 80910
719-574-1150
Fax 719-574-9840
Website: www.wsusa.org

Of Related Interest from Continuum International

Alfred Adler, Anna Freud, C. G. Jung, and Others, **German Essays on Psychology,** edited by Wolfgang Schirmacher and Sven Nebelung

Also includes W. Dilthey, Edmund Husserl, Erich Fromm, Karen Horney, Wilhelm Reich, and many others.

John Bayley, **Hand Luggage: A Personal Anthology**

A famous writer and critic, in many ways best known as the husband of Iris Murdoch, presents the "internal dialogue" he maintained during his wife's deterioration from Alzheimer's Disease.

Dr. Raymond B. Flannery, Jr., **Preventing Youth Violence: A Guide for Parents, Teachers, and Counselors**

"This book is essential for those who work with children in any capacity." —Library Journal

Sigmund Freud, **Psychological Writings and Letters,** edited by Sander L. Gilman

Includes letters to Fliess, "On Dreams," "Infantile Sexuality," "The Uncanny," and more.

Margaret Kornfeld, **Cultivating Wholeness: A Guide to Care and Counseling in Faith Communities**

"A state-of-the-art guide for all who minister today."—Catholic Library World

Meira Likierman, **Melanie Klein: Her Life and Word**

The first major study of his important figure in British psychoanalysis.

Richard Nelson-Jones, **Theory and Practice of Counseling and Therapy**

A new edition of the highly regarded text that reviews the major theories of counseling and psychotherapy, explaining their practical applications in working with individual clients.

Tom Shakespeare, **The Disability Reader: Social Perspectives**

The first anthology of academic writings on disability studies.

Tom Shakespeare, K. Gillespie-Sells, and D. Davies, **The Sexual Politics of Disability: Untold Desires**

Jean Vanier, **The Scandal of Service: Jesus Washes Our Feet**

A beautiful meditation by the founder of the first l'Arche community, devoted to the lives of severely disabled individuals.